NOT BORN YESTERDAY

"How to avoid canine pregnancy pitfalls, rearing regrets and puppy homing headaches."

Sara Lamont

Published by
Elite Publishing Academy
www.elitepublishingacademy.co.uk

First Edition published 2019
© Sara Lamont 2019

Printed and bound in Great Britain by
Elite Publishing Academy

A catalogue record for this book
is available from The British Library

ISBN 978-1-912713-29-5

To my mutts, past and present.

The ones who broke my heart when breeding, Stella, Patsy and the little 'LaRoyals' who weren't strong enough to make it.

It's for them this book is written for, if I can help one breeder avoid these tragic situations, then it's been worth it.

Contents

What Breeders and Pet Professionals have said about Not Born Yesterday 11

PREFACE 13

Everyday Breeders 13

Deutsche Großmutter...14

Potty Mouth Pooches...14

INTRODUCTION 17

Breeding Blind Spots 17

Proactive breeding...19

CHAPTER 1 - Breeder Bond..21

Breeder Oath...22

Observation - Oath...23

Acknowledge the problem - oAth 24

The Balance 24

Signs of Pain...24

Breed-specific pain thresholds...25

Take Action - oaTh 26

Finding a font of all knowledge...26

Help - oatH...27

Breeder Game Show..31

You make the final decision 31

CHAPTER 2 - Condition or Illness..33

So what changes might you see in the early stages of pregnancy between mating and five weeks gestation?..33

Marred methods to determine motherhood 35

Method One: Human pregnancy kits...36

Method Two: Gums going pale at around 21 days 36

Method Three: Nip pics..37

Method Four: Human foetal heartbeat Doppler 37

Accurate Pregnancy Confirmation...38

CHAPTER 3 - Pregnancy Preparations...41

Supplements 41

Worming & Flea treatments 42

Vaccinations 43

Exercise 44

Diet 44

Stress 45

CHAPTER 4 - Breeder Friendly Vets 49

Changing with the times 50

Multiple vets for Multiple reasons 52

Birthing Plans 53

Making Decisive Decisions 55

No decision, or action, is still a decision. 56

Planning minimises risk 56

CHAPTER 5 - Budget Breeding 59

Penny pinching puppy play toys ideas 62

Whelping Setup 63

Infinity equipment 64

CHAPTER 6 - Birthing Plan : Natural Delivery 67

PLAN A: Delivery of puppies at home 68

Signs of labour - Stage 1 68

Developing Labour - Stage 2 69

Delivery 71

Stuck pup 73

Puppy Revival 73

Cord-cutting 74

CHAPTER 7 - Birthing Plan : Surgical Delivery 77

PLAN B & C 77

Plan B 78

Plan C 79

The Waiting Room 79

Solo pup protocol 80

CHAPTER 8 - 4 Phases of Puppy Progress 85

Phase 1 - Vital : 0 to 2 weeks old 87

Puppy defects 87

The science 88

Puppy checks 89

First Feed 91

Puppy Identification 92

Mum Checks 93

Mastitis 94

Eclampsia 94

Every day's a school day 95

Poorly pups 95

Treatment 96

Hand rearing 97

Bottle Feeding 98

Syringe feeding 99

Sponge feeding 99

Tube Feeding 99

Puppy Loss 100

CHAPTER 9 - Vetting : 2 to 4 wks 103

Why bother with socialisation? 103

No fear! 104

Sound Therapy 105

Worming 106

Weaning 107

Putting the feelers out 108

Questionnaire / Vetting form 110

Your Qualifying Criteria 111

Declining enquiries 111

Next stage: Telephone Call 112

Next stage: Waiting List 112

Next Stage: Puppy Viewing 113

Deposits 113

Deciding on a price 114

Payment methods 116

CHAPTER 10 - Phase 3 - Viewings : 4 to 6 wks 119

Puppy Socialisation 119

No Likey, No Lighty 120

Puppy Protection 123

The importance of chipping 126

So what are your options as a breeder? 127

CHAPTER 11 - Phase 4 - Venture : 6 to 8 wks 131

Vet & Vaccinations 132

Puppy Collection 133

The Puppy 134

The Puppy Information Pack 135

Sales Contract 136

Worming regime 137

Puppy's microchip number 137

Puppy Pet Insurance 137

Feeding advice 138

Treats 139

Toxic & Poisonous 139

Registration details 140

Parentage Information 140

Vaccination Certificate 141

Toilet Training 143

Exercise information 143

Training information 144

Grooming information 145

The Basics 145

External Parasites 146

Coat Types 146

Professional grooming 147

Socialisation information 148

Additional Extras 148

CHAPTER 12 - Prevention is better then cure 151

Female Cycle 151

'Morning after' medication 152

Chemical Castration..152

Permanent Choices 152

CHAPTER 13 - So that's it 155

J.F.D.I..155

Want more help? 156

ABOUT THE AUTHOR..159

Moi? 159

Acknowledgements 161

What Breeders and Pet Professionals have said about Not Born Yesterday

"Your book is soooo good. I'm loving it. I love the tips on security and vetting potential puppy owners. There were tips I'd never even thought of, but alarmingly that's the reality we have to be prepared for."

Ashely Ware *(Discobull's Show Kennel)* - New Breeder

"The book is really well written, sensible, enjoyable and understandable."

Kathy Senior BVM&S GP CERT (SAM) MRCVS - Veterinary Surgeon

"This book is very informative and clearly structured. Useful tips on supplements and what to look out for, with regards to warning signs and the dog's health. It walked through each stage and was clear and to the point, no waffling."

Nicky Greve - New Breeder

"Great simple explanation for new and established breeders, a lot of which many, I'm sure, do not always consider. I think this is a very well needed book. Obviously I LOVE the fact you've included the importance of breeders carrying out appropriate socialisation of their pups."

Mandy Locks *(Akira Dog Training)* - Professional Dog Trainer & Behaviour Consultant

"This book covers simple and complex things that many people might not think of — my favourite chapters where the Birthing Planning (Plan A, B & C) and the 4Vs.

11

I find these incredible, so vital for people and full of information. I've only bred a few litters and am a newbie but these gave me so much more that I have ever thought of."

Monet Rennison *(Zaniah Show Kennel)* - Novice Breeder

PREFACE

Feeling sick as a Dog about your possibly pregnant Pooch?

This book isn't your usual 'dog breeding book', I don't lecture or preach about whether you should breed your bitch or why, yes I dropped the B-word, but in 'dog land' this isn't a swear word.

This book focuses on the proactive steps you need to take. Firstly in accurately confirming pregnancy and if positive, what measures then need to be made. Puppies bring with them newfound accountability, which will most definitely be inherited by you, as the Breeder.

Yes, that's right, you are a Breeder.

It's not a dirty word, I know I've been called worse.

If you raise a litter of puppies, you are viewed by others as a Breeder. Whether you feel like one or not, whether you like the 'label' or not, that's what you are.

Pet dog owners seem to have this idea of a Breeder being some superhuman person who lives rurally, was born into a family that coexisted with animals for centuries and went to some sort of 'Dog Breeding University', graduating with first-class honours.

Everyday Breeders

In reality, they are muddling along like us all, dealing with life and the curveballs it throws us. While juggling the things that are precious to us, family, friends and our pets. Being a breeder is just one part of you, how big this segment of you grows will depend on the frequency you breed and your natural interest to do the job properly.

13

Don't be mistaken, anyone who buys a puppy from you will consider you a Breeder, and they will have particular expectations.

All of which will be covered in this book.

Deutsche Großmutter

I was raised by a straight-talking English mother of German descent, like many mothers she had her 'phrases' and 'the glare' would keep my brothers and me in check, particularly in public.

I remember being prompted by my mother "Pick your feet up!","Share your sweets or wait until they've gone home" and "speak up or shut up". It was also drummed into me "You do the best you can". No matter what the task was, it was to be done to the best of my ability. Not in a pushy mum way.

I've approached all my dog activities with the same vigour, starting with ownership, then to exhibiting, followed by breeding, different committee and officer roles at breed clubs and achieving highest show judge status in my 30s. Along the way carving my career as the 'Canine Family Planner', helping thousands of breeders by providing services to fulfil their breeding dreams and aspirations.

Which ultimately lead to me to start writing. Some people might call me an author, I certainly don't feel like one, but if there's a published book with my name on, I guess I am. Equally, if there's a puppy you've reared and carefully homed, you're a Breeder. I hope you see the similarities?

The question is, what type of Breeder do you want to be? One who's naive, scared and anxious? Or one who feels prepared, confident and in control?

Potty Mouth Pooches

If your dog could talk you probably wouldn't need to read this book and the task of breeding would become easy. They could tell you exactly how they are feeling, what their daily struggles are, what would make them more comfortable and if they felt under the weather and needed to see the vet.

I know for a fact if any of mine could speak, I'd probably have a potty-mouthed one, like Mark Wahlberg's childhood toy in the movie Ted. As I write this is yet to happen, so we Breeders need all the help we can get.

Come to think of it, I do call one of my dogs 'Poohy Poppy', and you could consider her 'foul-mouthed', but it's certainly not because she can talk.

This book walks with you through every stage of breeding, helping you to avoid pregnancy pitfalls, rearing regrets and puppy homing headaches. I share with you a vast amount of knowledge and experience plus tips on how to apply it.

It's widely recognised Bulldogs are considered one of the hardest dogs to breed, I certainly wasn't aware of this when I started on my own journey. When you've been through many peaks and troughs of breeding, it certainly provides you with information and advice to help others avoid the same situations.

This book doesn't just include my own encounters, but information gathered from my peers and colleagues, pet professionals, veterinarians and the largest pool of all, my clients. The foot soldiers on the ground; all types of Breeder and breeds - pedigree and mixed. These are real people, just like you, doing the best they can, tackling the same problems and issues.

This resource is to be read cover to cover, more than once if needed. Don't be precious about this book, crack the spine, turn the corners of 'interesting' pages and make notes by scribbling in the margin. It's brimming with simple but effective ideas and actions to ease your breeding struggle.

You'll gain insight into safely whelping your female, rearing her brood and how to place them into their 'lifelong' homes correctly.

This care and consideration will set you apart from other breeders, fundamentally galvanising your breeder ability. If you want to fast track your breeding knowledge, then the **Home Breeder Hub** could be for you.

www.caninefamilyplanner.com/NBY

The Hub is an online resource centre, filled to the brim with tools and tip to support you on your breeding journey. There's a stack of downloads, audio and video goodies you can access instantly to get you started with your puppy planning.

INTRODUCTION

Breeding Blind Spots

It was late October and still unusually warm, even though the leaves had turned brown and were dropping from the trees. I was walking two 4-month-old Bulldog puppies, Poppy and Norma, from my most recent litter.

They loved attempting to chase the leaves being pushed along the pavement in the fresh autumn breeze. The wind had created neat piles of leaves to form naturally in pockets along our path. One of the pups dived in with much enthusiasm and was neck-deep in the mound.

I thought it was probably how many dog owners felt when they start their breeding journey.

They often tell me they feel up to their necks with worry, concern or anxiety from the unknown of what lies ahead. These feelings are amplified when you receive positive confirmation your dog is pregnant, and you'll soon bear the responsibility of hopefully numerous little bundles of new life.

I advise any owner suspecting their dog 'maybe' pregnant don't put yourself through the pain of not knowing. Find out as soon as possible so you can start preparing, there's no need to keep guessing otherwise you could be in for a nasty surprise in 9 weeks, this is how long dogs are pregnant for, just over two months, a 63 mere days. In reality, these dates can vary, and pregnancy can be as short as 57 days or run slightly over, up to 65, so the important thing is not to be caught short.

Typically by the time owners start suspecting something they could already be nearly halfway through the pregnancy, meaning you might only have 3 or 4 weeks. Not even one paycheck to get organised.

In a past life, when I was a Learning & Development Consultant working for various corporate companies, I used to train the 5P's of planning in management workshops.

1. Proper
2. Planning
3. Prevents
4. Poor
5. Performance

I prefer the 6 P's - Proper Planning Prevents Piss Poor Performance, to drive the point home. Either way, the bones of the model encourages you to suitability consider, think and act on a situation helping you avoid problems, drama and unnecessary emotional stress. Concerning dog breeding, you have the possible related vet expenses too.

So I created my own 7P's.

1. Proper
2. Planning
3. Prevents
4. Problem
5. Pregnancies &
6. Poorly
7. Pups

I'll tell you now, it's the premise of this whole book. I'll highlight tonnes of points which you need to consider and act on if you want to increase the chances of stress-free breeding experience if there is such a term?

I believe you should always assume breeding will be a positive experience and everything will go well and with ease, but preparing 'a plan' helps you to make concise and informed decisions with confidence.

When I learnt to ride a motorbike, one of the first protocols I was taught was a slightly adjusted 'mirror - signal - manoeuvre' it was 'mirror - signal - check - manoeuvre'. Check your mirror, signal but before manoeuvring, also glance over your shoulder to check your blind spot.

Weirdly I now also do this when driving in my car, I only rode 500 miles on the bike before I sold it. It was apparent to me the UK weather and my hairstyles were not bike-friendly.

This quirk always appears when I'm joining from a slip road or changing lanes. It's just become a safety habit and one I'm happy to keep. The 7P's are the same thing, a mantra which will always prompt you to check your breeding 'blind spot'.

Proactive breeding

---

proactive[proh-ak-tiv]

Adjective: serving to prepare for, intervene in, or control an expected occurrence or situation, especially a negative or difficult one; anticipatory.

This book isn't going to bog you down with the analysis of the anatomy during pregnancy and birthing; it emphasises the importance of animal advocacy, all the step's that underpin this practise, so it becomes a natural part of your breeding routine.

This book deep dives into birthing plans, the importance of having the right medical professionals supporting you, rearing techniques, following the Breeder OATH, 4 phases of puppy progress, your breeder responsibilities and why correct puppy socialisation is vital.

This book covers the stuff no-one ever tells you, but people 'in the know' are doing.

It's perfect for first time breeders, breeders who want to improve their current routine or just want a refresher and for stud owners to help support bitch owners.

Not Born Yesterday

Laying down the sturdiest of foundations when it comes to dog breeding and feels a fitting way to consolidate, while commemorating, my twenty years of breeding.

Cin-Cin!

And here's to twenty more.

CHAPTER 1

Breeder Bond

I'm going to point out the obvious, being female I never made the 'grade' to join the Scouts, and the Brownies never seemed to appeal to me. I did join colour guards, basically flag-waving, for a period of my life. We used to tour the UK to perform with a Scouts marching band in the summer, and without them during the winter.

I always wanted to join the band to play the snare drum having come from a musical background of playing the flute and the saxophone. My guilty pleasure to this day is a film hardly anyone has watched called Drumline starring Nick Cannon, aptly based around the American phenomenon of marching bands.

I never had to take the Scout's Promise or Oath, but I totally get the importance of the practice. Taking an Oath seems a bit of an archaic ritual by today's standards, but when said aloud in front of witnesses, it becomes a powerful statement for all to hear. This is no doubt why the practice still happens at significant times or important places like court, at a President's inauguration and even marriage vows.

The Boy Scout Oath

On my honor, I will do my best
To do my duty to God and my country and to obey the Scout Law;
To help other people at all times;
To keep myself physically strong, mentally awake and morally straight.

'On my honour, I will do my best', something instilled in me and echoed through all my activities, not just dogs and a fundamental principle for this book. I like to think as part of our human nature we are all striving to try out best, but sometimes we do like to tell little white lies to ourselves to feel better.

'To help other people at all times,' I like to think this isn't exclusive to mankind but also includes mammals, such as our trusty canines.

'To do my duty to Dogs', sorry I misread, it does actually state God. 'and my country and to obey the Scout Law'.

Part of the Scout's Law is poignant 'A Scout has courage in all difficulties.', you may experience difficulties when breeding, and you will most certainly need to have perseverance in bucket fulls.

Breeder Oath

Declaring an oath of your intended behaviours and actions is compelling and no doubt why the practice still exists today. Even the Scout's oath resonates with me.

Supporting a bitch through her pregnancy is the best and most important role you can fulfil as a breeder. Your canine companion will rely on you every step of the way. When necessary, you'll need to reassure her and support her through experiences and emotions she might not instantly understand.

Your role during this pregnancy is to act as the spokesperson for your dog. Being the animal advocate when required. During your girl's pregnancy, you should be making daily checks as part of her whelping wellbeing.

A proactive breeder continuously monitors her health and condition, the adage 'Prevention is better the cure' supports this attitude.

When breeding goes well and to plan it's a joy, however you are not genuinely tested as a breeder until you've experienced some 'turbulence'.

This is when your well thought out schedule starts to veer off track, and the decisions you make will decide whether you can pull it back or not.

Breeding always involves an element of risk, you can help to minimise the risk by planning and preparing.

The Breeder Oath isn't an oath as such, the word itself will act as a prompt to help you recognise potential issues during your breeding journey, highlighting when to escalate them.

- **O - Observe** her daily; Is she in good health? Eating, drinking and sleeping ok? Is she struggling with the pregnancy?
- **A - Acknowledge** If there is a possible problem or issue. what do you think is causing it? Is she in pain?
- **T - Take action** to maintain or improve her condition. Is there a simple or fast solution? What can you do to make it better? Make her more comfortable?
- **H - Help.** If none of your interventions have improved her condition, you need to seek professional veterinary advice, who will be able to medically diagnose the condition and put a treatment plan in place.

Let's look at each area in a bit more detail.

Observation - Oath

More experienced breeders will have the knowledge of their own historical breeding experience, plus examples and stories from their canine network and research gained from books or the internet, but there is no 'Dog Breeding Uni'. Knowledge is accrued over time in many ways, all taking effort.

Sometimes there is no right or wrong to some of the experiences you'll go through, contrary to what you may see on social platforms hosting whelping groups.

In these places, you'll frequently see people arguing what's the right or best way to do something. There rarely is a right or wrong, black or white answer; breeding is more like every shade of grey.

You know your girl when she isn't pregnant, so how is she different now?

Acknowledge the problem - oAth

The Balance

Attempting to balance the symptoms of a problematic pregnancy, long term health of your female and the viability of the puppies she is carrying is a balancing act. Your opinion and next actions may vary depending on the breed of dog, your existing knowledge and your personal tolerance to risk.

Your bitch's health is your utmost priority, followed by the survival and health of her pups and at times it will feel like you are walking a tightrope.

Let's be clear and have the conversation no one wants to have. Your bitch is your primary concern and any puppies come secondary. Most females never asked to be mated, and therefore her life is your responsibility.

Breeding is not risk-free, but little is. If you are lucky, you will never experience any of the most challenging parts of breeding.

If you become a frequent breeder, you significantly increase the probability, and if you are really unlucky you might experience it on your first and only litter, who knows?

Signs of Pain

It's essential to identify pain; this will help you recognise when the balance isn't in your favour. In isolation, these observations are no major cause for concern, but if your female is suffering two or more of the symptoms. Then you need to progress to the next step, and take action.

- Restlessness or difficulty finding a comfortable position

- Vocalizing (whimpering, groaning, crying)
- Decreased appetite
- Less desire to interact
- Excessive licking, biting and scratching a body part
- Sleeping in an unusual position or in an unusual location
- Panting or trembling when resting
- Unusual aggression when approached or touched
- Changes in eye expression (starring, dilated pupils, vacant look, squinting)
- Teeth grinding
- Sickness/vomiting of water or food

Breed-specific pain thresholds

If you've ever visited a medical facility with a complaint of 'pain', they've probably asked you to rate it on a scale of one to ten. One being no pain at all and ten being the worst pain imaginable.

This question is typically challenging to answer because unless you are someone who has dealt with a good variety of pain, you could be rating a cold as high as an 8, it's probably unlikely to help the doctor.

Animals are no different, even if they could talk, this time it still probably wouldn't help you. It's widely recognised some breeds have different pain thresholds.

The breeds of a more 'stubborn' demeanour, evolving from a baiting/fighting background tend to have a higher tolerance to pain.

This means you could have less time to 'take action' or 'seek help', meaning the whole experience can feel a lot more dramatic and decision making can feel rushed. You need to be able to gauge and establish how critical she is realistically.

Take Action - oaTh

If you get to this phase, it means you need to 'do something' to maintain or improve your female's condition. Depending on time sensitivity, you may need to research what options you have, contact people in your 'canine network'. These might be breeding peers, mentors or other animal professionals, including your vet.

Finding a font of all knowledge

If possible, have someone you can refer to for advice and talk through your thought process. Ideally, the person is not involved with the immediate situation, level headed and has breeding experience, but they don't have to have the same breed.

It's also worth asking the stud owner or the breeder of your female if they can mentor you. Maybe a retired breeder or even a local reputable breeder.

Mentors are hard to come by as it takes time, patience and the ability to share by teaching in an 'unbiased' capacity. People are moving online to seek support from communities active in breeding, whelping and rearing such as Facebook groups.

While these are great for initial researching, at times, information can be conflicting and provided by individuals who lack any creditable breeding experience. Better still you might want to check out the Home Breeder Hub, this is an online resource and community I manage that is full with tried and trusted advice. Check it out at **www.canienfamilyplanner.com/HUB.**

If you are following the birthing plans I recommend in this book, you will have already established a good relationship with your vet, and they are typically a more direct and effective route to seeking answers. If the situation is time-pressured, the only action you need to take is to contact your vet.

If the issue is non-critical and you find a solution to your problem, and you observe a satisfactory improvement, then you don't need to move to the next stage. You will still need to observe her frequently.

If you have tried some recommended remedies and you feel the improvement is not satisfactory, or you find no remedy then you must progress to the next stage.

Help - oatH

Following the OATH framework helps you clearly identify and express your concerns to your vet, including any measures you have already taken.

They will have additional provisions which can help you during this crisis; firstly they can accurately diagnose having the medical knowledge, equipment and experience to do so. The ability to prescribe the best options to maintain or improve her condition, which could include medication or even surgery.

It's your responsibility to understand the information they provide and the options you have. Make sure it's clear you and your dog's rights and needs are respected.

Make sure all treatment choices have been exhausted, not just the quickest or easiest. A mutually agreed option should be the safest for her and the puppies. Have the confidence, if required, to challenge procedures or practises if you feel they are not suitable.

The 5 W's & 1 H are an excellent system to follow to help you gather information to make informed decisions; this style of questioning is used by news reporters:

Who? What? When? Where? Why? And How?

If you are not happy with the advice you've been given, remember you can always seek a second opinion. You'll rarely ever need to do this, but it's always good to remember you have this option.

I have previously walked out of a vet practice refusing them to operate on my dog with primary inertia after I was told the dog would have to be spayed and the puppies will probably die.

In less than an hour, I was at different practice 35 miles away for an elective section with a fully recovered non-spayed dam and her two healthy babies. I had a tough decision that day, and I went with my instinct.

Patsy Case Study

An example of OATH in action, even after twenty years of experience.

Patsy was a 2 year old, fit and healthy dog. She was Bulldog Breed Council health tested and until her season was training in the basics of Flyball. A pretty rare sport for this breed, but she loved jumping and playing due to her natural athleticism, which is not totally untypical for the breed.

This was Patsy's first litter, and she was mated to a stud I had previously used and had an outstandingly consistent litter of nine pups. She had the same sire as the previous Dam's litter, so I expected the type produced to be much of the same.

Up until 50 days gestation, Patsy was still keen to go out for road walks and seemed to be blooming in her pregnancy. I had pregnancy scanned her and knew she as carrying a fairly large litter of eight.

Day 51 gestation Patsy didn't look right, her belly had gone hard, taut like a drum and very, very round, which was my first **observation**.

Day 52 Patsy didn't want to eat, kept being sick (weird brown fluid), was wimping as she moved and was finding sleeping very uncomfortable. All these **observations** pushed me to **acknowledge** this as not normal pregnancy behaviour, and I **took action** and took her to the vets for **help**.

My vet offers an outstanding independent out of hours service, but there is a 45min car journey each way.

At the vets Patsy was x-rayed, ultrasound scanned and had full blood work ran. Nothing. We didn't have a clue, she was put on a precautionary course of antibiotics, and administered an anti-sickness jab to make her more comfortable and improve her condition.

Day 53, Patsy had eaten a minor amount of food but was still suffering sickness. I **observed** her condition had not improved overnight, so I took her back to the vets the following morning.

We agreed, we needed to get her to day 57 gestation and c-section early. She was given a painkiller and another anti-sickness injection.

By 12pm that evening here had still been no improvement, she was still unable to eat, drink or sleep. I phoned the vet and confirmed I was bringing her in for an emergency section. Our two previous interventions had not maintained or improved her condition.

With reluctance, they agreed and by 2am (on a bank holiday Monday) Patsy was prepped for surgery. 8 puppies born, but expected (and accepted) they were too underdeveloped to survive, two of the pups were deformed. Because of the early c-section, the puppies were not ready to detach from the uterus, which caused internal bleeding. Patsy was also spayed.

It was gone 3am, and I was hoping to be heading home with her, but the vet wanted to keep Patsy in for observation. Only at this point did the vet confirm I had made the right decision.

At 11am I returned to pick up Patsy, she walked out the practice no problem. After a few days of home recovery, she was back to her normal self (if that ever existed). She never produced milk (too early) or seemed depressed about having no babies; I don't think she even realised she was pregnant.

This experience with Patsy cost me over £3,000, but what was way more important was that Patsy was alive. After some research it seemed she was suffering Maternal Hydrops, it's pretty rare and fortunately not something many breeders experience. She just seemed to look and feel a darn load better than a few days before.

I don't tell you this story to scare or frighten you. Breeding isn't all doom and gloom. Bizarrely this experience is the breeding success story I'm most proud about. I have no doubt many breeders would have lost Patsy, trying to get her to day 57 of gestation, and not wanting to compromise the puppies.

So I feel I really cut the mustard by following the OATH model and moving between all the steps, numerous times gave me great confidence of what to do and when.

I would do exactly the same, all over again.

Patsy at 7weeks gestation.

Looking bonny carrying my 29th litter that was never meant to be.

Breeder Game Show

You make the final decision

We've all watched them game shows when nearing the end of the programme, after a whole episode of gameplay, the players have the toughest choice to make.

Leave now and go home with a tidy sum of cash and prizes, or double it to be crowned a gameshow winner. We all wonder how confident, or greedy, they are going to be!

Not many get their cake and eat it. Mo Farah remains the only person in the UK to get the full £250,000 from The Cube, and Judith Keppel remains the only female winner of a handful, to bag the entire 1 million from 'Who wants to be a Millionaire'.

You too will have some difficult decisions to make during your own breeding game show. There is no one size fits all when it comes to breeding and you certainly never stop learning, every bitch, every pregnancy and every litter is different.

The experience can be made significantly easier if you carry out a few preventative and straightforward checkpoints along the way by acknowledging the Breeder OATH.

If requiring veterinary assistance, the options involve the loss of puppies, the litter or spaying; this only confirms the complexity of the pregnancy, which is potentially life-threatening. Without question, for the sake of your female, you act in her best interest and should agree to such measures.

This is THE hardness decision when breeding, but ultimately there is nothing more devastating than ended up with nothing.

A breeder mantra is "If in doubt, get them [puppies] out".

I would much prefer to regret the decisions and actions I made, then the ones I avoided or postponed. You making the decisions means you are in control of the situation, and this is the only way you will learn as a breeder.

But let's not get ahead of ourselves, we don't need to worry about such things unless we know for certain our dog is pregnant. So what's the best way to find this out? Keep reading...

CHAPTER 2

Pregnancy is a condition, not an illness, or is it?

I can recall my sex education classes while in Secondary school. The boys and girls were split into separate classes, and 'the vitals' were explained to us. I'm sure some of the kids, even-aged 14, could teach more than the teachers. Anyway, the one main takeaway I had from the lessons was:

"If you have unprotected sex and get pregnant count yourself lucky!"

There was a considerable emphasis on STDs, and you only have to watch 5 minutes of 'Embarrassing Bodies' to put you off your dinner, and sex, for life.

Like I mentioned before if your dog could talk, you could give her a real good grilling of what she's got up to the other night when you came home to find a jailbreak of the cage or baby gate which was safely keeping her and Romeo apart. No doubt she'd be grounded.

Instead, it sometimes comes down to the owners' sixth sense or watchful eyes, identifying initial signs of possible pregnancy. These observations of changes are what typically sparks their 'possible' pregnant antenna, suggesting the little pitter-patter of puppy paws may be on the horizon.

So what changes might you see in the early stages of pregnancy between mating and five weeks gestation?

I am asked a lot about the signs of pregnancy and whether I can guess if a girl is pregnant before she's ultrasound scanned for confirmation.

My answer is always no.

Until the ultrasound probe has made contact and I see puppies, I never even contemplate trying to guess whether a female is pregnant. In the past, I have fallen into the trap, like many, of thinking they are, or they aren't, and it turned out to be the opposite.

Signs of pregnancy may include loss of appetite, some females will possibility display morning sickness. Generally, this is caused because their hormones are whizzing around their body making significant changes to prepare for the pregnancy.

The hormone Progesterone is present after ovulation and is required to maintain a pregnancy. It has also been associated with an upset stomach, regardless of confirmed pregnancy. The issue is these types of conditions are also the same symptoms of a dog being ill. If prolonged or in excess, you must seek veterinary advice to identify any underlying problems.

Another common observation is the female becomes attentive and clingy. She always wants to be around people or her preferred owner. She may want her belly to be rubbed or prefer not to have her belly touched. You won't always know whether this is due to pregnancy or pain due to an undiagnosed condition.

She may also become more lethargic, not wanting to get out of her bed or on her usual walks, or not for as long. A dog looking unwell, not wanting to do their usual routine, can also be a sign of illness rather than pregnancy.

Maiden females, who have not previously had a litter, will show little physical indication of pregnancy before 35 days gestation. It's been known for the Oestrogen hormone to aid water retention, which can visually change the shape of your dog. In particular around her undercarriage and the vulva (most pet owners tend to call their foo-foo!), these changes are due to hormones not due to pregnancy.

You may have heard about teats becoming bigger and rosy or changing shape and sagging more. These changes can also occur with phantom pregnancies. A phantom is where a female displays all signs of being pregnant, even up to the point they produce milk, but they're not.

A change in body shape and weight gain could also suggest a possible womb (uterus) infection, such as closed Pyometra. Caused by the build-up of pus in the uterus, causing her to gain weight, causing a pregnancy 'looking' body shape.

Pyometra could also be the reason for her being lethargic along with possibly a raised body temperature, panting, loss of appetite and an increase in drinking, as she's trying to flush her system of the poisons.

Discharge is typical in pregnancy, and a small amount is to be expected, a clear discharge after mating is not a problem. If the discharge is foul-smelling, murky in colour or could be described as 'strawberry milkshake' looking, then this could be open Pyometra. An open uterus infection will have noticeable pus starting to drain from the body.

I must stress, if you suspect your female may have Pyometra then seek veterinary advice immediately, this is a time-sensitive condition of which your female will only deteriorate over time.

Hopefully, I've provided you with enough examples as to why it's so essential to make sure you confirm if your female is in pup. As I learnt from my sex education lesson, pregnancy is most certainly better than an undiagnosed illness.

So what methods are available to confirm pregnancy?

Marred methods to determine motherhood

There are many ways to waste your time and wonga on different techniques, wondering if your dog is pregnant. I'm sure you'll see many 'bright' ideas while researching online.

Method One: Human pregnancy kits

Have you seen the recent craze on social media were the wife or girlfriend reveals to her partner that she's pregnant by leaving the pregnancy test kit somewhere for them to find? While the entire revelation is filmed.

I always thought it would be a wicked trick to play on your partner and before they reach new levels of concern say "ha-ha don't worry, it's not mine; it's the dogs!" -- an easy way to prank them and break the news that the dog is having a litter.

Well, it wouldn't work, and the prank would be over.

Why?

Because you can't use a human pregnancy kit on dogs. There is a canine version but requires a blood draw, not urine.

Most vets won't stock these kits, and more importantly, they can give incorrect negative results up to 33 days pregnancy, by then you can ultrasound scan providing more accurate information.

Method Two: Gums going pale at around 21 days

It's something to do with the blood rushing to the uterus, so it takes it away from the rest of the body.

I don't believe there's any medical evidence to confirm this is an accurate way of confirming pregnancy. Even if it was, it's not going to give you an idea of the number of pups to expect, or the possible gestational date.

Even if you take a picture of the gums before and after to compare, how do you know it's in the same light, at the same angle with the same period before or after exercise or food which will speed up her metabolism, increase body temperature and blood flow changing her colour. Meaning to many variables make it easy to miss.

Method Three: Nip pics

You'll see this plastered all over social media with comments like "Does my dog look pregnant?"

Who knows? Because who knows what they looked like before-hand, Linda?

Old school methodology is teats will become more pronounced and rosy pink. This will be more difficult to ascertain on a female who goes through these changes but is having a phantom pregnancy, or long-haired breeds.

I'm going to group palpation here too. Generally only advised if a trained person practises it, which means a vet, by feeling around the abdomen. I feel there is little accuracy, even if they are reasonably confident she is pregnant; still, the numbers are a total guestimate.

Method Four: Human foetal heartbeat Doppler

This equipment amplifies the sound of a potential puppy heartbeat for you to ascertain whether she's in pup or not.

The problem with this is the quality of the equipment along with the quality of gel, and the skill of the person. You'll find it's hard not to pick up the mother's circulation, picking up her heartbeat through various arteries running through her body. You'll hear a lot of swishing and white noise which can be misread as puppy heartbeats.

I had a client use this equipment in the later stages of pregnancy when pregnancy had already been confirmed by other methods. They were then panicking because they couldn't find any puppy heartbeats and were concerned they may have died. On further investigation, they were all very much alive.

Foetal heartbeat monitors are in the same bag as the Draminski pregnancy detectors. I believe they run on the same kind of principle. If you don't know what this device is, I wouldn't bother spending any time to find out.

So in summary, don't bother wasting your wonga, or your time, on human pregnancy products or even substandard dog ones.

Accurate Pregnancy Confirmation

You can use an ultrasound scan from as early as 28 days from the last mating if the person conducting the scan is experienced. This doesn't necessarily mean a vet. A skilled technician will be able to provide you with accurate information about pregnancy and puppy development. To know if they are skilled ask when booking if they can:

- Identify the correct size for gestation?
- Identify if the puppies have the correct development points?
- Confirm how many puppies they have seen?
- Advise on other general observations?

Later gestational scans can define organs, observe limb movement, skull and body can be measured for size and provide due dates estimates.

Not only is it possible to confirm the gestational status of the puppies, but also the an approximate number of puppies expected. The more skilled the technician, the more confident they will be in providing numbers.

Nothing is 100% in life, well apart from death and taxes, but scanning is going to give you a damn good idea of what's going on and help you plan.

Scanning can also pick up things, which are not necessarily problematic but untypical, such as empty gestational sacs or the absorption of puppies.

All of this can also be offered in the comfort of your own home. There has been a recent boom in mobile breeder services and fertility clinics assisting at your convenience and ease. These individuals should be highly skilled, experienced and insured in all the services they are offering. If in doubt check, by seeking other breeders opinions or reviews.

Small businesses offering pregnancy scanning, are more likely than your local veterinary branch to have newer equipment and the confidence of frequently conducting these types of scans.

A skilled, trained eye may discover other underlying health issues. They can't diagnose but will refer you to your vet. I've found bladder crystals, usual artefact's such as cysts and masses, pelvic kidneys and closed pyometra.

I want to mention X-raying quickly. This method is common practice in America where ultrasound scanning is highly underutilised. X-raying can only be carried out in the latter stages of pregnancy when the puppies bones have formed. During this time, ultrasound would provide similar information much sooner without x-ray emissions. For this reason, they probably should be avoided to prevent any damage to the development of a foetus.

I always liken breeding to gathering parts of a jigsaw puzzle, the more pieces you collect, the clearer the picture becomes.

Confirmation of pregnancy is just one part of the puzzle; there's many more to come during the whole experience.

The next chapter will provide you with a few more puzzle pieces to ensure you and your dog bloom during her pregnancy.

CHAPTER 3

Pregnancy Preparations

I remember as a child being forced to take a supplement every morning; I can't remember exactly what it was, I assume some form of multi-vitamin.

I'm not sure why my brothers and I were given it, whether it was a fad or the family doctor had advised it. I also recall being given cod liver oil, to help us I become more intelligent. I'm yet to appreciate if this has any long term benefits.

I kinda feel the same way about canine supplements; if they're fed a good quality complete food, I don't see the need for supplements unless you have a particular reason to do so. Generally, their food will provide all the nutrition she might need.

A slight tweak may be needed in the later stages of pregnancy depending on the breed and litter size.

Supplements

The Royal Canin research team did a study to see whether dogs benefited from Folic Acid supplements. They confirmed folate supplementation particularly for flat-faced breeds (brachycephalic) such as Pugs, French Bulldogs and Bulldogs significantly reduced the risk of cleft palate by nearly 50%.

They recommended giving 5mg per day, 15 days before mating until puppies are born. For the cost of this supplement, I think you would be crazy not to supplement your girl if from brachycephalic heritage, as rearing puppies suffering cleft palate can be challenging.

Raspberry leaf is commonly used by breeders; some people say it's able to improve the tone of the smooth muscle of the uterus, aiding the dog's labour. This supplement will benefit females who are giving birth (self-whelping) naturally.

I currently use in the final weeks of pregnancy SF50, a dietary supplement which ensures a correctly balanced supply of essential nutrients helping to keep your dog in good condition, especially during periods of stress and when lactating.

I find this helps to prevent her coat dropping (fur falling out) due to lack of condition while she's feeding puppies. Helping her avoid looking ropey when it comes to new owner puppy viewings.

Worming & Flea treatments

Treating parasites only when seen maybe the wrong approach, particularly when you are planning to breed. Regular maintenance and observation as part of a routine care plan will help prevent any unexpected issues. If you are planning to mate your girl, then I would worm pre or early season as part of your preparation. There are a fair few safe flea treatments for pregnant dogs, including Frontline (Fipronil based) or Bravecto (Fluralaner). You may wish to seek veterinary advice before administering any.

There are also more old skool methods such as the nit comb, I mean flea comb and cleaning the home environment and boil washing all soft furnishings if infested.

The majority of vets will recommend that you worm your dog around 40 days gestation, when pups are formed and when the puppies are 2 weeks old to prevent the transfer of worms.

Panacur is typically recommended, its active ingredient, Fenbendazole, is deemed safe during pregnancy. This product does kill Lungworm, but not at the dosage given for pregnancy. Milbemax or similar products, if provided monthly, will treat Lungworm, but there are no safety studies into the suitability during pregnancy and lactation.

I had an insightful conversation with a canine worm count company, similar to horse testing, at Crufts a few years back.

They explained the issue with worms possibly becoming resistant to chemical wormers and future problems that may arise if we continue to overdose and treat dog's indiscriminately rather than checking to see if they 'actually' have worms.

They recommended that instead of fretting about which wormers are needed and when instead test your girl to see if she has worms at 40 days gestation.

Should the result be positive, then you can specifically treat the type of worm, instead of the blindly trying to treat all.

They then recommended testing the puppies when they are 2/3 weeks old, which involves collecting a sample of poo. If positive, you treat puppies and mum, if negative then no treatment is required.

You then carry out one final check when the puppies are 7 weeks old of which certificates can be provided for your new owner puppy info packs, detailing the puppy's worm status.

I thought this a super way to ensure you're not putting too many chemicals into the mum or puppies and is a lot more effective at treating the specific parasite they may have.

Vaccinations

Puppies inherit a great deal of health and immunity from their mother immediately following birth until around 14 weeks of age. Ideally, your girl is up-to-date with her annual boosters or has been titre blood tested. Confirming she has sufficient immunity levels against the most common highly contagious infectious and fatal viral diseases such as Distemper, Parvo and Hepatitis.

It has been suggested, even with lapsed vaccinations, it's acceptable to delay Boosters until after the puppies are born. The dam will still have a level of immunity from previous vaccines. Vaccinating while pregnant can negatively impact the unborn puppies immunity.

Exercise

I don't believe there is any need at 35 days (5 weeks) gestation to restrict her exercise when initially confirmed in pup. I would exclude her from any rough play with other dogs and restrict any jumping.

She will soon tell you when she wants to limit her exercise, so don't force her when this time arrives. Restricting her access to unknown dogs will help reduce the risk of any contagious infections such as Kennel Cough. Inform any dog walkers, daycare and groomers early in the pregnancy, so they can advise you accordingly.

Diet

Many owners follow their own personalised feeding regimes. Owners of working kennels and/or breeds tend to make minimal changes to the food type or quantity until puppies are born, apart from splitting meals into smaller portions.

Preventing overfeeding helps avoid large puppies and the associated issue of getting stuck during birth. Once born, she can eat all she wishes to produce high-quality milk, for the pups to thrive. It's said raw red meats such as lamb and beef plus a Fenugreek supplement help milk production.

It is a myth feeding milk, goats or puppy supplement will to help the mum produce more milk. She just needs some high-quality food and plenty of fresh water. Feeding her milk will help her maintain her condition due to the ease of ingesting a high-calorie content fluid, but not produce more.

Transferring to the same brand of food but the Puppy variety in the final 2 weeks of pregnancy is widely accepted. This offers a higher nutritional quality in the same quantity of food, alleviating any uncomfortable full tummies when carrying large litters.

Some breeds will transfer to a complete wet or raw food if previously fed kibble for the final weeks of gestation to reduce the likelihood of 'water puppies'.

These puppies retain water and are oversized or jellified, some breeds are more prone to these than others. It's believed they created partly due to high sodium diets and research is considering a combination of parent particular blood types. These breeds include but not restricted to Bulldog, Mastiffs, French Bulldog, Pug & Boston terriers.

A note should also be acknowledged regarding the feeding of raw meat, all fresh foods should be suitability handled and hygiene dealt with the most seriousness. Infections like Salmonella or parasites like roundworms are significantly increased with raw feeding practises.

This is a very high-level summary of the initial consideration's that should be made during your dog's pregnancy. These initial actions start to form more vital parts of the jigsaw puzzle, helping you to cultivate a problem-free pregnancy.

A female will gain around 25-30% of her body weight during pregnancy with an average size litter for her breed. If you are unsure of how much when to increase her food and by how much then check out the free 'Dam's Diet sheet' and video available in the Home Breeders Hub at **www.caninefamilyplanner.com/NBY**.

This breeder help sheet will help you keep track of her dietary changes and demands during pregnancy and also while she is weaning puppies.

Stress

One of my dogs is not overly keen on walks; in fact, she is usually petrified. She hides under the dining room table when she knows it's walkies time and I have to coax her out. On the walk, she is hyper-vigilant scared of every person, gate, lamppost or poo bin.

Sadly, I can't even pinpoint the turning point of when this behaviour became the norm.

I'm no dog trainer but what I have learnt is, at some point, my dog has experienced a perceived threat or danger while on a walk, and she goes into survival mode. You know the one; fight, flight or freeze. She freezes and then I persist on the walk which she completes in full flight mode. She'll do whatever she can to get home as fast as possible.

When a dog is in this mode (or even humans) stress hormones are released to help them 'deal with the situation', heartbeat increases, eyes dilate, muscles are supplied with energy so they can act fast, e.g. run away or fight.

Once the danger is gone, the body should restore to normal, which can take up to 72 hours. A problem can arise when the threat is persistent. Trigger stacking is when the body doesn't get to fully recover because additional threats are experienced.

The body is continuously elevated and under stress. Stress is tiring, and as we know for humans, long term has negative impacts. Dogs under long term stress can be anxious, have behavioural issues, vomit, suffer diarrhoea and have thinning of the coat and skin outbreaks.

When dogs stress hormones levels are elevated, energy is redirected from vital organs shutting down the digestive, reproductive and immune systems while stopping growth. Meaning stress can have a direct impact on fertility, pregnancy and unborn puppies.

In 2013, researchers at the University of Edinburgh led a study investigating the link between stress hormones and stress-related behaviour of newborns animals.

They found Cortisol (stress hormone) can cause the mother's placenta to shrink, directly affecting the developing brain of the foetus due to the reduced flow of nutrients.

Furthermore, the researchers proved increased exposure to Cortisol resulted in smaller pups, and these animals went on to exhibit the signs of mood disorders.

The research also showed how stress or trauma might impact the genetic character of a pregnant mother's unborn pups.

The concept supports stress can not only impact a females fertility but also her pregnancy and the unborn puppies she's carrying, which could even affect them in later life.

This highlights how vital it is for you as a breeder to know the signs of stress, decipher the triggers for each individual dog and ensure they are managed, particularly if the dog is in your breeding programme. You'll need a robust puppy socialisation to prevent the triggers being passed on for generations, but we'll cover this a little later in the book.

These concerns do nothing but highlight the importance of having only dogs of sound temperament within a breeding plan. Producing puppies who develop into well-adjusted adults with their new owners, both living a long, happy and contented life together should be the aim.

I've covered extensively the negative impact stress can bring to your dog, but what about you? Well you already have the Breeder OATH and 7p's to guide you, but you can't do this on your own. All successful people, in just about any walk of life, have a supporting team around them.

So who should be in your team? I've already highlighted the importance of having a canine community with breeder expertise, but you'll also going to need an outstanding relationship with a team of handpicked veterinarians, not just one. You'll find out how to do this in the next chapter.

CHAPTER 4

The importance of a suitable vet

I had been struggling to find the type, fit and style of trainers I wanted, so I decided to splash out and buy a pair of Nike iD.

These are when you design and customise a pair of trainers online. You can be very specific with the detail, such as material and colour for every part of the shoe, sole and laces, even the air bubble.

I decided with winter fast approaching, I'd go with a base colour of black, figuring they wouldn't show any dirt and black goes with everything, right?

I'm going to confess I have relatively large feet (for a lady) and rarely have the choice of girly pinks or purple footwear, so I ordered them with a pink Nike tick and few other 'pink' highlights.

Mostly a black and pink trainer.

They arrived fast and fitted like a glove. I was really pleased with them.

After a few weeks, I realised I hadn't particularly worn them. I liked them, I designed them. They were comfy and ticked all my requirements, and for over £125, I should want to live in them.

Then I realised it had a made a booboo, my ingenious idea of having black trainers for the winter was the flaw. How often do I wear black? I don't.

I live in navy blue or grey, mainly because the dog hairs show less. Doh!

They simply didn't match any of my clothes. I decided to purchase another standard 'off the shelve pair' in grey, slightly cheaper but only just.

I've lived in them ever since. I should have made my iD's grey and pink, not black and pink. A minor but significant difference.

You can easily fall into the same kind of situation with your vet. They look like a vet, act like a caring professional but are they the right vet for you in this current situation?

I've dedicated a whole chapter to drive home this very, VERY important point, so it shouldn't be ignored.

Initially, you picked your vet, most probably because they were the closest to you, offered an excellent puppy introduction plan or seemed competitive on price or value for money. They ticked all your boxes - at that time.

But you now need to take a step back, like I should have before I ordered my trainers and looked at the bigger picture, or my complete wardrobe.

Changing with the times

Things have changed for you and your expecting canine mum, how would your vet practice meet your new needs and requirements?

One of the most important steps is to make sure you have a "breeder friendly" vet.

This is a vet who will not get judgemental or feel inconvenienced when you start asking questions in regards to your dog pregnancy. You need to have these conversations early in the journey for you and your girl to avoid any pitfalls as the pregnancy develops.

Don't leave it to the point where you or your dog are in distress, seeking help, but not getting the information or support you need or expect.

You are now seeking a vet with not only breeding experience but within the overall pro-breeding attitude. They should be able to support and guide you through the experience and provide expert clinical care.

You have a choice.

You must remember, effectively your dog has private health care, you have the pick of any vet at your expense.

You don't have to be tied to only one practice. You may find a practice which provides proper puppy health checks and vaccinations, but a local vet more suitable for everyday bits and bobs such as wormer and flea treatments.

You may choose to use a third for breeding related aspects because they offer their own out of hours service and have excellent continuity between their vets.

There should be no issue with you doing this.

You'll need to find a vet in your vicinity, who can confidently offer you reassurance during the pregnancy and birth. You should be able to rely on them if required, in and out of hours.

You need to do the homework now, should any drama arise for your dog. This is a massive step to avoiding them in the first place.

Now don't be mistaken, according to the Royal College of Veterinary Surgeons (RCVS) guidelines, you can't "officially" have accounts at lots of practices. They believe the treating vet might not have the most relevant up to date clinical information on your dog, this is a more than fair reason.

From my experience, this will only become apparent, or an issue, if records need to be shared. I would assume the female being bred has a minimal clinical history reflecting her excellent health and vitality. Otherwise, it questions why she is being bred.

51

If you have a dog with an ongoing illness, and medical records which need to be shared for consistency of treatment, then this approach is not suitable nor may it be for pets with insurance cover.

Multiple vets for Multiple reasons

I currently use four different veterinaries practices, in the perfect world, I would need only one. You might be lucky? If you can find a practice you can trust, a team of vets you respect and who respects you then read no more and skip to the next chapter. If you aren't sure then personally I would encourage you to build your own team:

1. One for convenience as they are on the same road I live in.
2. Another because they offer extended opening hours at no extra cost.
3. Another because they are brachycephalic (flat face) specialist and breeder friendly with outstanding out of hours services.
4. Finally, another who's exceptionally competitive for Puppy health checks and vaccinations and annual treatments for my adults.

I'll admit it's taken me many years to build this quadrant of veterinary professionals, who I'm now happy with. You'll need time to develop your own triangle or quadrant.

If you are eligible for low cost or free vet care from PDSA, they strongly recommend getting your pet neutered and would advise against breeding from them.

As a charity, they will not use their resources to support any breeding practices and will expect you to take the pet to a private vet for any treatment relating to pregnancy or birth.

They will always provide life-saving treatment if a pet's life is in danger because of pregnancy or birth, however, once the pet is stable, you'll be referred to a private vet for any further treatment.

Your vet needs to be kept in the loop once your girl has been confirmed in pup, you should contact them with the news. Ensure they pencil her due date in their calendar, so they are aware you might call them for advice or services.

Specifically ask to speak to your preferred vet directly, avoid the receptionist relaying 'messages' as this can end up like a game of Chinese whispers.

Even better, pop in branch to meet them face to face, especially if you are a new customer, and have the conversation about your concerns/situation.

Birthing Plans

Just because they are a veterinary professional does not make them an expert on canine reproduction, notably the husbandry side. Ask about their plans regarding your biggest concerns, this might be:

- Confirmation due dates
- If she goes overdue?
- What support do they offer out-of-hours?
- Approximate cost, including out of hour charges?
- How can cost be minimalised?
- When is payment expected?
- What're their experiences with arduous labours?
- How experienced are they with c-sections? Do they advise of any special precautionary treatment for particular breeds or situations?
- What's their opinion of breeders?
- What's their stance on elective sections?
- Protocol with Solo litters
- Do they prescribe antibiotics and painkiller after a c-section
- What's their advice on the use of calcium and oxytocin to support problematic labour?

Ensure your conversation includes all 'birthing plan' options. Hopefully, her whelping the pups at home is first choice (Plan A), but

53

have the conversation before it's needed if Plan B is required (c-section in hours) and Plan C (c-section out of hours). I'll cover this in much more detail later in this book.

Confirm her due date, typically 63 days from ovulation or 61 from mating (but can vary from 57 to 65), so they can check staff availability for assistance.

If they don't sound suitable, have the confidence to ring around. Speak to other breeders in your area (any breed) and other animals professionals such as your ultrasound technician or even groomers to see what vets they recommend supporting owners when breeding.

If you don't know any breeders, then use Google and make contact explaining your predicament and asking them what vet they recommend or use. You may find they all gravitate to the same one for a good reason.

I recommend you update your vet, 2 -5 days before her due date. Check the provisional plan is still applicable and discuss any concerns you may have. The last thing you want is any drama or emergency assistance, so again discuss all options in advance.

Sara's Suggestion:

All pet owners should register with their local vets inside the popular pet stores like Pets at Home. These practices have much more flexible opening times than most.

They tend to open earlier and stay open later, ideal for working owners, and offer full trading hours on the weekend and during the bank holidays, where other practise's would class this as 'out of hours' treatment and would be considerably more expensive to access.

All your efforts into finding the right vet could be diminished if you require out-of-hours assistance with somebody who has no or little knowledge of you, your dog or your circumstances.

I personally avoid any veterinary practice which doesn't provide their own out-of-hours, for any emergency assistance when breeding related. I would stay clear of any vets who ask you to transport your own dog to a central, shared out-of-hours practice.

Making Decisive Decisions

Many moons ago I had a credit card with American Express, an Amex card. I'm not sure why I had an Amex, as so many places don't take them in the UK due to the higher processing charges for the retailer. I think I was acquiring Nectar points when I used it and we all know, points mean?

Prizes!

I was much younger and naive; I had piles and piles of unopened post. I was never concerned about unopened statements as I always paid my bills. Until one day I went to use the card and to my embarrassment, it was declined, I was horrified and suffered the usual 'check out' humiliation.

I knew for a fact I had, an available balance in the thousands. I got home, and I logged onto to my account online - "SUSPENDED".

I phoned them to find out what the issue was.

'Miss Lamont, have you not responded to the letters we've written to you?'... 'Ergh, no?' as I glanced as the piles of unopened letters.

The crucks of it were having been a customer of nearly 10 years apparently I needed to re-validate my salary and I.D. They had written to me numerous times asking, and of course I had failed to reply.

No drama I thought, I'll just send them the info they needed.

'Sorry Miss Lamont your case has now been referred to the debt collection agency.'

Wow, just wow was my response. Well no, it wasn't, it was much more obscene.

So my failure to open my mail had nearly resulted in me getting a massive black mark against my name with a credit card I didn't really want or need.

What did I learn from this?

No decision, or action, is still a decision.

I had decided not to open my mail, and this had a consequence. My inaction was still a decision, and ultimately, it comes to bite me on the bum. I learnt a big lesson that day, and now I live a more organised life with even a 'mail-in' system.

I also carry this lesson with me when breeding, I know if I don't find the right vet, if I don't check the bitches temperature or I don't feed the pups at a particular time there will be consequences.

When it comes to breeding I'm proactive; I want to find the potential problem before it's even occurred because this attitude saves puppies and brood bitches lives.

Planning minimises risk

In 2015 a few friends and I decided to try our hand at dog shows in Europe, the World Dog Show it's the Crufts equivalent for Europe was being held in Milan, Italy.

It took meticulous planning of transporting four people and three dogs during the warmer climates. The trip had numerous 'challenges' including breaking down in Germany, thankfully we had full Eurotunnel breakdown cover and was given a much higher spec vehicle then we were travelling in, to continue our journey.

We made it to the hotel, to walk out less than an hour later. A frantic online scrabble found us a more suitable place, paying for accommodation twice, we did return the following day to request a refund which resulted in the Polizia, yeap that's right the Police being called.

By the end of the first night, all three of the woman had cried. The icing on the cake was after getting into bed, I had realised I had lost both my dogs pet passports, which meant they wouldn't even have access to the showground let alone been shown or even been able to get back in the UK We've travelled over 900 miles to fall, at what felt the final hurdle.

Thankfully with some clear thinking of Chris, the only male accompanying us. We returned to the first hotel at 2am in the morning for security to allow us to look in our original rooms, there they were in the wardrobe.

We finally made it to the first show (of three) and realised none of us had eaten for over 24 hours. We had all been so stressed by the experience, we had failed to ensure our basic needs were met. We were in 'fight for survival mode', fighting every step of the way to make sure the journey was a success we had planned.

We had a successful trip with some good wins and lots and lots to reminiscence about, good and bad.

When I decided I fancied attending the same show a few years later, but now being hosted in Amsterdam and the possibility of travelling a fair distance on my own, I was prepared.

I had a plan A, B and C. I checked the hire van had fully working air conditioning, I checked with the hotel to confirm my room was on the ground floor and had 'adjustable' air-con.

I downloaded an app, so I could be GPS tracked by family, I pre-booked my dog in for her wormer with a Dutch friend vet so passport entry back to the UK would be no issue. I ensured I went to the show venue the day before, knew the carpark access and quickest way to the show and I pre-programmed all destinations into my satnav, and the dog even had her own suitcase with all her essentials.

I had another successful year with much less stress, and I certainly didn't miss a meal this time.

Proactive planning minimises risk.

Remember, *Proper Planning Prevents Poorly Pups & Problem Pregnancies* and taking the time to consider every possibility, regardless or not of it actually happening. Helping you to deal with these issues, empowering you to make decisions with assertiveness.

When it comes to breeding, I recommend everyone has a plan A, B and C.

- **Plan A** - Self or free whelp at home, possibility needing veterinary assistance if required.
- **Plan B** - C-section 'in hours' also known as semi-elective section with no major drama.
- **Plan C** - C-section 'out of hours' also known as emergency section typically, accompanied with concern for life of pups or dam.

Hopefully, you won't need these plans, but like any corporate business, it's wise to have a disaster recovery plan. A set of tools and procedures to help execute the continuation of services.

You need to talk through all these options with your vet, step by step. This will help you avoid any nasty surprises which could end up being an emotional or financial catalyst.

Talking of money, you don't need to spend a fortune to safely breed and rear quality puppies, find out in the next Chapter what 'Infinity' equipment is, and why I prefer it when organising a whelping setup.

CHAPTER 5

Budget Breeding

So as a birthday treat to myself, I decided after too many years to book myself in for a MAC makeup tutorial. With an up and coming wedding (not mine) I thought I need to go 'back to school' and learn about some of this 'stuff'. I'm not a girly girl, so makeup as never been particularly on the top of my important list.

Having listened to friends' comments, I was prepared to splurge around £250 on the occasion. I was well out of my comfort zone, as I stepped into the shop with mirrors on every available wall space. I learnt a lot on my crash course session, including preparation was vital, that message felt kinda familiar. I also discovered I needed more than one tub of foundation powder and who knew you needed four eye shadows for just 'one look'.

Once I was happy with my 'final face' I was asked if I wanted to purchase any of the products. I said I'll take the lot, I had zero idea of what any of these products cost.

Retrospectively I could have had a quick gander on their website before my visit, but it was a treat, and I had the cash. I didn't even have a quick browse walking past all the products to the makeup counter for my appointment.

25 items were run through the till and makeup tutor Tammy said 'That will be four twenty', so I thought well that's not £4.20 it ain't even £40.20 no she means £420.00! Wowski! It didn't even include a mascara.

I paid up, and thought I wonder in training if they get taught not to say 'hundred'? I learnt a lesson that day, if you are on a budget, then you need to put effort into knowing you aren't overspending.

I could have made an effort to educate myself on the cost of these products before I even left the house. I could have saved money by looking at competitors and not purchasing in the moment. However, I did none of this, and I paid for the convenience and privilege.

Breeding is no different, it will cost you money, and you need to have an idea of cost, so you aren't stung like me. A general rule of thumb is to allow the sale of one puppy in the litter to cover whelping and rearing costs.

The most significant cost being a possible c-section bill. Some vets even request you prepay these expensive bills before offering treatment. Some breeds are more predisposed to them, but factors such as litter size (big and small), size of the sire, the size and overall condition of mum and owner experience can all increase the chances of a c-section.

Typically the more expensive the puppy, the more likely they are born by c-section or they are much more time-intensive to rear.

For example, in some breeds, the mother is not left unattended with her pups due to her clumsiness, short back and thickset body. The Breeders generally keep the pups in a heated 'puppy box', every 2 to 3 hours this will stimulate them to pee and poo. Then watch every puppy suckle for at least 30 minutes, before putting them back and doing the same all over again in 2 hours, for at least 10 times a day for the next 10 days.

Some would call this a form of torture?

Some call this breeding of the most intense nature. While other types of breeders can just glance in the whelping box daily to check all is ok.

The following preparations will also take you a long way in the prevention of you parting with your precious pennies and saving puppy lives. There will be times when there are no compromises, and you'll just have to bite the bullet and cough up the coins.

Thrifty tips to help your Breeding Budget

Ask for a discount or if there is a 'breeder discount' available, especially when purchasing puppy related items, particularly if you're a regular shopper or you'll need to buy multiples of them.

For puppy vaccinations etc. some places will provide a 10% discount on the listed price if you don't ask you'll never know.

You must be careful about changing the dams diet and food when in pup, the last thing you want is to cause an upset stomach. Traditionally it's advised to put the female on the puppy variety of her existing food. When feeding the pups to help maintain condition, this same food can then be used to wean the puppies, meaning you don't need to buy lots of different brands or types of dog food.

It's worth looking around and contacting the food manufacturer to see if they offer a Breeder Scheme or Club. Also, some food distributors offer Breeder discounts for bulk buying.

The Breeder Schemes typically provide you with puppy packs to supply to the new owners, including a sample of food or a voucher to purchase the food locally with various other Puppy information leaflets, measuring cups and containers.

It's certainly worth shopping around as some brands will not only provide the puppy packs but also the food for you to start your weaning. This isn't just limited to kibble, I've seen complete raw companies offer great deals too. The food you wean onto should be the brand you would typically use or buy, and the new puppy owners will continue to feed.

Some breeds may be fed a particular food until 6 - 9 months to support their rapid growth pattern and then moved on to an entirely different brand of food. Typically of a much lower protein level and considered 'maintenance' food. This isn't a problem as long as it's clearly explained to the new owners in your puppy packs.

There is an opportunity to earn rewards and sometimes money by providing your puppies with free insurance for their new homes. This helps to raise the new owner's awareness of the importance of ongoing pet insurance but also offers you short term coverage for any unforeseen illnesses or accidents at no cost to you.

The insurance companies are generous in offering this temporary form of coverage, in the hope the puppy owner will become a long term customer and continue the cover after the free period has ended.

If you don't plan to breed regularly, then you may not want to have the considerable expense of purchasing puppy equipment. You can re-purpose items or ask friends and family if they have any specific equipment you could use, which they no longer want or are happy to lend to you.

Sourcing second-hand equipment from the Facebook marketplace, Amazon, eBay, Freecycle and Gumtree is a great cost-effective way to pick up some bargains, which you can still sell after use.

Hire equipment may also be another option for you. There are premium whelping setups with additional oxygen concentrators costing over £1,500 to purchase, but these can be hired for a fraction of the price.

This saves you the initial outlay, especially if you are not sure if you are going to be a frequent breeder, avoiding the need to have storage space for the equipment when not in use or sourcing re-placement parts.

All types of equipment can be hired, including puppy boxes, incubators, puppy pens and whelping beds all delivered and collected from your front door.

Penny pinching puppy play toys ideas

Sometimes the simplest things in life are the most enjoyed. This can undoubtedly be the case with puppy toys. You can spend a small fortune on expensive pet store toys. But my suggestions may bring just as much, if not more, for a fraction of the price.

Toys are essential for a well-reared puppy, not only as a source of entertainment but as a critical component to a well-socialised puppy. We'll cover the importance of this in more detail in later chapters.

- The trusty cardboard box - Easily obtained, the heavy-duty double-walled type tend to last longer. Puppies enjoy hiding in them, standing on them, chewing them, sleeping in them. You could even upgrade to a plastic 'toy' tub and a little bit of bedding to make a 'day bed'.
- Kitchen roll tubes (or larger) - The puppies love the ability to pick up and run with this cyclical tube. Which soon get siblings wanting it too. Alternatively, a toilet roll with an old cotton sock fed through and knotted at either end makes a simple cardboard dumbbell.
- Fizzy pop or squash bottles - Remove the label, lid and tamper band. Puppies will have hours of fun chasing this light, audible, bouncing bottle around. You can also put some dried pasta in the bottle and recap to add some additional excitement.
- Small plastic vitamin bottles - Small empty plastic bottles filled with some dry rice gains, wrapped in a cotton sock makes for an enjoyable tug of war toy.
- Soft Toys - Check out your local charity shops or keep an eye on the Facebook Marketplace for used children toys such as play gyms or child-friendly soft toys and tunnels.

Whelping Setup

Once pregnancy has been confirmed, you have permission to purchase.

Your expecting mum will need an area of privacy where she can whelp the puppies in a calm environment. The area should be large enough for her to lay fully stretched out comfortably, with a heat source such as a heat pad or lamp.

The area should be easy to clean, whelping and pups can be a messy business, so wipeable surfaces are preferred. The area should have easy access for the Dam to step in and out, but for no puppies to be able to escape.

It should also be easy for you to lean into and assist when necessary, so no crates or cages. People with DIY skills may be able to build something suitable after a few Google searches. For the rest of us, there are many options and choices to research and purchase.

Infinity equipment

I must admit I'm most certainly not a morning person, but naturally a night owl. I certainly don't struggle to do the puppy 3am night feeds. I'll happily stay wake to 1am on a school night, due to FO-MO (fear of missing out). I'm not exactly sure what I might be missing out on, but I'll sacrifice sleeping hours for it. When required I'll be up the next morning early to walk the dogs, work or a dog show.

In the summer months, this is easy, the sunshine peeping through the curtains tells your body there's nothing else better to do then get up and enjoy the day.

However, during the winter keeping this enthusiasm can be a stretch. One of my biggest challenges is finding dog poo in the dark, the dull amber street lights don't seem to help in the long-overdue, uncut grass.

I've historically used my mobile phone torch. It can be tricky holding the phone, two leads and picking up poo. I've used a keyring torch dangling from a leash, and I'm now even considering a beanie hat with a LED light sewn in, who I see joggers using. Ultimately they all do the same thing, but it's finding what works for me and my street cred.

Having these options available is no different from the choices you'll have when building your first whelping setup. There is no right or wrong to what you should include; the two main factors will depend on the size of the breed and the size of space you have available.

Personally, I like to keep things simple and where possible, use the same equipment in multiple ways. A bit like the infinity scarves and dresses that can be worn a hundred different ways, okay a hundred is slightly exaggerated but you get what I mean. Having equipment with flexibility to be used numerous ways will help as the puppies transition through differing growth phases.

For example, you can buy or make a whelping bed and then up-grade to a puppy pen. I always recommend people purchase a freestanding heavy-duty metal puppy playpen and use it for both purposes.

For whelping the sides should be lined with cardboard, cot bumpers or anything which can be cut to shape and wipeable to stop any drafts or puppy limbs being trapped in the rungs. They generally come with trays reducing coldness from the floor and are wipeable for hygiene.

I cover half of the top opening with a secured towel, to provide a darker, warmer, snug area and play whale music. Okay, I lied I don't play whale sounds, but the bed should be in a quieter and calm area with a lower family footfall or visiting traffic for some privacy.

Rails can be made to prevent puppies from being squashed against the sizes using poles or dowel. A heat lamp can be easily secured across the top, though my personal preference is a heat pad as they don't dry the air and are easier to control due to the direct contact temperature. If pups get hot on a heat pad, they can move off it; it's harder for a puppy to avoid heat cast from a lamp if too close.

At 4 weeks, the pen can be transformed like a mini-episode of DIY SOS. Rails removed, the area can now be filled with play and potty areas. Once the litter is said and done, the Puppy Pen can be easily collapsed and stored or sold as they are highly sought after.

If you don't know where to start, you can download a copy of my 'Whelping Wish list' and watch the supporting video in the Home Breeders Hub at **www.caninefamilyplanner.com/NBY**.

This breeder help sheet lists all the items you may require for your breeding journey but also categorises the objects by their purpose and if the item 'essential' or a 'nice to have'.

However, I can tell you one of the items on the detailed list.

A notebook and a pen.

Why?

Think of your notebook like the patient observation clipboard. These used to sit at the bottom of a patients bed when in hospital. Any care assistant would read your notes before even attempting to treat you.

That's why it's so important to write stuff down, especially if the caring duties for the litter are shared between two or more people, but also to relay information to the vet.

You should write all and anything which may be relevant to this pregnancy and any future litters. We are just mere mortals and easily forget things.

The 'forgetting curve' is a real thing. This model estimates we can forget up to 90% of what we learn within the first month.

Most breeders don't have a litter a month for 12 months a year, so we all forget stuff, it's natural too. You don't need a photographic memory, but you should be able to recall this information using notes correctly. It's this organisation which adds to your breeder experiences and supports the OATH framework.

I'm sorry to break the news, but your puppies won't arrive by stork or DPD courier, so you best keep reading to suitably prepare for their arrival.

CHAPTER 6

The Birthing Plans

I'm not going to deny it, I really like the convenience of buying 'stuff' online, and I love even better, getting parcels delivered. I am probably really addicted. Not knowing what's inside most the time, as I've totally forgotten what I've ordered. Usually, it is really dull and mundane items. Dog food, interdental toothbrushes, printer labels or clothes which don't fit.

I really like DPD couriers, you are always kept informed of where the parcel is, they text a delivery time within a 30 mins time frame, and you can even track your parcel en-route to you.

That's niffy stuff if you ask me.

If only puppies were delivered the same way. A GPS tracked update, as the stork drops them off to your doorstep. No such chance.

Most people's closest experience with birthing is watching 'One born every minute' or 'Lambing Live' or indeed being the creators of their own children. They are far too distracted to observe and pay attention to the technical aspects of the birth, and then apply them to their impending canine birth.

Giving birth is a natural and beautiful experience, and effectively your role during the delivery is to be your girl's antenatal partner.

You need to keep cool, calm and collected which with all the OATH traits, shouldn't be an issue. During the birth, make sure you praise, reassure and encourage her and when required, make sure she's comfortable and relaxed.

So what is the plan?

- **Plan A** - Self or free whelp at home, possibility needing veterinary assistance if required.
- **Plan B** - C-section 'in hours' also known as elective section with no major drama.
- **Plan C** - C-section 'out of hours' also known as emergency section typically, accompanied with concern for the life of pups or dam.

So let's look into each one a litter further...

Plan A: Delivery of puppies at home

This is the type of birth most dog owners envisaged when they started on their breeder journey — picturing a perfect scene from the early 90s farming TV programme 'Darling Buds of May'.

Obviously, your dog has read the 'Easy Birthing Book' or this one, and follows it to the T, but we all know in reality your dog can't talk or read, so it's unlikely to happen.

In the introduction of this book, I explained, I'm not going to cover the micro details and technical process of puppy birthing. You'll find that in other dog breeding books.

I will cover the major practical points you need awareness too, helping you make decisions on how to best act for your female.

Signs of labour - Stage 1

Labour can start as early as 57 days of pregnancy, so make sure your whelping box is set up well in advance. Pregnancies are typically 9 weeks from ovulation. If you didn't ovulation test, you could potentially have a window of between 57 to 65 days gestation.

A drop in your dog's body temperature is typically the first indication of the first stage of labour. Once the temperature has dropped below 36.5°C, which generally sits around 38.3°C or there is at least

1°C from her average temperature. Remember you might miss the drop, it's a piece of the puzzle, not the complete picture.

Once it starts to rise again, you approximately have 12 to 24 hours before the whelping of a puppy. The increase in temperature also indicates the next, 2nd stage of labour. This is an ideal time to book an appointment with your vet for 36 hours later; if the labour progresses as you've planned, it can be cancelled. If it doesn't, then during this appointment, you may discuss the suitability of Plan B.

Your girl may start showing some of the following characteristics which are typical for labour, but not all do.

- Pant, shiver and show general restless
- Vomit or refuse food and water
- Nest by tearing up and move around bedding in her whelping box

I wouldn't recommend allowing her to eat at this stage. Excess food has a high possibility of it being vomited if a c-section is needed; this can impact the anaesthetic dosage. A preferred alternative is to provide freshwater or a hydration solution.

Developing Labour - Stage 2

During this stage, the cervix begins to dilate, and uterine contractions begin. These contractions can be painful and perplexing. She may quieten down and stop panting as if listening to something. This is a sign of contractions - write the time in your notebook.

Within a few hours, she should start to push actively. Amniotic fluid (yellowish) may be released, and the bitch may be anxious to lick it up. There will be a fair amount of discharge and it will vary in colour from clear to green.

The presence of green-black discharge, before the birth of a puppy suggests a placenta has detached. If this happens when there are no contractions, you must contact your vet immediately. If you see green spotting during active labour, there is no need for concern.

If contractions do not increase in strength or seem half-hearted in several hours, contact your vet regarding possible uterine inertia.

There are two types of inertia. Primary is when there are no or only partial contractions, they've started then weakened or stopped. Meaning the puppy will not be expelled normally through the birth canal. If there are no contractions at all, the labour can't progress. There are several reasons this may happen:

- Some breeds have a predisposition to the condition.
- A large litter and the uterus is overstretched, so can't contract.
- A small litter and the uterus is not stimulated enough.
- Puppies are small and not applying enough pressure on the uterine wall and cervix to trigger contractions.
- The Dam is overweight or lacking the muscle condition to contract correctly.

Secondary inertia is when the muscles become exhausted after prolonged contractions due to an obstruction. This may be incorrect puppy positioning, oversized puppy or prolonged birth due to a large litter.

From the point of heavy active pushing, a puppy should be present within 30 minutes. Each puppy is enclosed in a sac which is also part of the afterbirth; it may present and retract until positioned correctly.

This is perfectly fine if intact and entire. If ruptured during the birth, the puppy will have a limited supply of oxygen, which if delivered slowly, could result in their death.

It's worth knowing a little about oxytocin.

Oxytocin is a hormone secreted by the body and has two main actions. The first is the contraction of the womb (uterus) while birthing and the second is the contraction of milk ducts, releasing milk to nursing puppies.

Oxytocin can only be administered by a vet to jump start contractions.

An oxytocin alternative, called Caulophyllum 30c is a homoeopathic remedy which is believed to quickly aid contractions and delivery. It must be given every hour as soon as contractions begin until the birth of all pups is completed.

Calcium supplements can also be given to help strengthen contractions if weak. It's crucial to note calcium should never be given during pregnancy, as it will trick the Dam's body into thinking it's producing enough and then produce even less.

You can purchase liquid calcium which absorbs into the bloodstream quicker. Capsules can be used or tablets from any Pharmacy or Health food shop.

Calcium before the birth of puppies should only be given if symptoms of pre-eclampsia are seen and with veterinary instruction.

Eclampsia can be fatal, symptoms can include head tremors, increase body temperature, panting, restlessness and muscle spasms occurring at any during motherhood. This condition can be easily identified with a blood test at your vets.

Delivery

"It's time to get warm towels and hot water!"

We've all seen the films where they've referenced this during a child home birth.

Why?

Hot water, boiling, in fact, was used to sterilise instruments and clean the area. A hot compress used to help soften the tissues and ease the pain for birth.

Warm towels were used to keep the baby warm and dry them after birth, and often warmed in the oven. To this day, hospitals now have towel warmers and still, use warm washcloths.

So now is the time to get your metaphorical hot water and warm towels.

Keep the whelping area dry and clean at all times, newspaper or puppy toilet pads can be easily changed to bedding once whelping has finished.

If you are partial to hand sanitiser, make sure it's alcohol-free or wear gloves, not the washing up type, the thinner disposal ones.

Each puppy is enclosed in a sac which is also part of the afterbirth. Make a note of any puppies born out of their sac, so you have an approximate idea of how many may be retained.

You may want to inform your vet of this information, they may prescribe antibiotics as a precaution, or administer oxytocin to help expel them.

It's not a huge problem and rarely causes an issue. Some Dam's do like to eat the afterbirth when given a choice, and there is no issue with allowing them to do this.

The interval between births varies; hopefully, she can keep to the pace of one puppy every hour, longer is fine if the labour is progressive. If heading toward two hours, get her stimulated with a short walk around the garden and some calcium, if there is a significant wait, seek veterinary advice with consideration to inertia.

You can provide your girl with a glucose solution or general hydration mix to help provide energy and essential nutrients during labour.

If she were ultrasound scanned, you'd have an approximate idea of the number of puppies to expect. This might not be exact, but if she settles down after the last pup, seems content to rest and feed then, it suggests she has delivered all puppies. You can have a gentle feel of her abdomen to see if you can feel any puppy-sized lumps.

If you feel she may be retaining a puppy, then seek veterinary advice for the best approach to be taken. Some may x-ray, others may opt for giving oxytocin.

Stuck pup

An incorrectly positioned puppy can get stuck and become an obstruction for other puppies. 40% of pups are born backwards, that's rear feet first. This is technically not a breach puppy and will not cause any issues, particularly if still within its sac.

A breach is when the hind legs are tucked under the body, other abnormal positions include a head folded back over the body. Lubricate a finger and feel for the ability to manoeuvre it into a normal position. You may need to push the puppy back into the passage to re-position.

Have a towel handy to help dislodge a stuck pup by pulling during a contraction downwards in the direction of her feet, rotating it from side to side.

Stillborn puppies are often poorly presented due to being lifeless and limp and may need assistance to remove. They can be pushed out by an alive puppy behind, resulting in two puppies being delivered.

Puppy Revival

Oxytocin is also known as the 'trust' molecule and enables not only physical changes but also behavioural. Studies suggest oxytocin has been demonstrated to play a role in pair-bonding of animals — for example, mother to her young. But even to you as you've have supported her through her whole pregnancy journey.

If your girl fails to act quickly to tear open the sac which encapsulates the puppy, she'll trust you instinctively enough to do it for her. Show her how don't be afraid to get involved and take the lead.

Tear the sac with pups head facing downwards and shake puppy downwards to help drain mucus from nose and mouth. Use an infant suction bulb if needed and a soft towel to wipe the facial area clean.

Stimulate the pup to breathe by rubbing them with a towel which will also dry them, remember them warm towels I mentioned earlier.

If a puppy is slow to respond, a vet can administer a fast-acting breathing stimulant such as Doxapram. Unfortunately, there are few remedies you can source without a veterinary prescription which will work as effectively.

Old school mentors may suggest Brandy. It's also been known for a puppy to need over 30 minutes of harsh rubbing before it took it's first real breath. So don't give up!

Cord-cutting

Some people panic about this as much as carving the turkey at Christmas. Some girls will naturally bite the cord and free the puppy of the placenta when they are consuming it.

I remember once playing tug of war with a French Bulldog who just wanted her mid labour snack, and I was still trying to cut the cord and suitably tie it off.

You can tie off with doubled layered cotton, dental floss or dip the end of the in Iodine. It will dry up and fall off in a few days.

I wouldn't fret over cord-cutting and tying. I know many breeders who leave Mum to cut them, and they don't tie them either.

Squeeze the cord and push any blood at the end of the placenta, back towards the pup and hold for 20 seconds.

Tear with a fingernail or cut with sterilised blunt scissors, remember what the hot water was for, about 1 inch away from the pup's body.

My preference is longer rather than shorter, but not too long otherwise it'll drag when they are moving about. Pulling may cause additional bleeding.

Well that's Plan A well and truly covered, but what about Plan B & C? If you are looking to avoid costly breeding bills, then read on.

CHAPTER 7

PLAN B & C

When we first started showing dogs, I was just 13 years old; it was my responsibility to get us to the show venue, as I couldn't share any of the driving. This was in the days before satellite navigation and finding a village hall on a sleepy Sunday morning, with no pedestrians to ask, was never easy.

I used to get the road map atlas the night before and work out every square was a certain number of miles, and with an average speed of 60mph, it would take a particular amount of minutes, then add on 30 mins for traffic and wrong turns.

We once followed a car with 'dogs in the boot', to their home and nearly ended up on their driveway.

Guess what?

They weren't going to the show we were heading for.

I was threatened a few times by my relatively short tempted mother, "that's it! We are turning back and going home." even though we were only 10 minutes from our destination after a three-hour car journey leaving at 5am.

Then sat nav was invented. I'm not 'that' old, but kids don't know how lucky they have it nowadays. My trusty sat nav even has live traffic updates and if needed, will redirect my journey to take a quicker route. Nothing feels smugger than driving on a parallel road, full of bumper to bumper traffic which you could have got stuck in.

You can get a similar feeling when you prepare for breeding, particularly if you have Plan A but going wayward meaning, it's no longer a viable option. Then just like a sat nav needs to reroute you to the same final destination. You need a Plan B and maybe even a Plan C to get you there.

Owners and vets sometimes need to resort to a plan B, this is typically surgery, a c-section, to eliminate birthing risks. Either the mother is at risk from developing a condition, complication, or to reduce the risk of puppy death. I define your options into two categories:

- **Plan B** - An mutually agreed C-section 'in hours' also known as elective section with no major drama or semi-elective if in early stages of labour.
- **Plan C** - A time-sensitive C-section 'out of hours', also known as emergency section typically, accompanied with concern for the life of pups or dam.

Plan B

Plan B may be an option considered for novice owners, bitches with previous inertia issues or suggested by a practice who doesn't have their own out of hours cover.

Other reasons maybe if the litter is extremely large or small, or factors such as public bank holidays might make Plan B a calculated and sensible choice.

This choice rarely comes without a significant vet bill and still has an element of risk. Most vets will not want to execute this plan unless the female is in 1st stage labour. Or you have identified ovulation and have confidence that any medical intervention is at the right time.

A c-section too early can result in the premature and underdeveloped puppies that are unlikely to survive. The placentas are not ready to detach, and forced removal can lead to haemorrhaging. Placentae should be left in place and passed naturally days later if the case.

Understandably, most vets are apprehensive when it comes to Plan B, so you need to make sure you are on the same wavelength and understanding. If you believe in the 7P's, you will realise the importance of finding the right vet and therefore will be in agreement.

The use of a short-acting steroid 2 to 8 hours before surgery can stimulate progesterone decrease, prevents shock developing and stimulates the lungs in puppies, making the success rate significantly higher for elective c-sections.

Plan C

Plan C is the last resort and really the plan you never want to experience. This plan typically kicks into action when you get chucked a curveball.

Maybe a puppy is oversized and becomes stuck, causing an obstruction or contractions have started to fail, and oxytocin hasn't been successful. At this point, you have significant concerns for any puppies and maybe also the dam.

If transporting your girl to the vets, don't use a crate or cage, neither are accessible or practical if she births a pup in transit.

Post-operation, if she's not on her feet and walking comfortably, it's usually better to place her in a strong blanket and with assistance lift her directly to your car with the four corners of the blanket.

The Waiting Room

I personally never leave my dogs at the vets and go home under these circumstances or plans.

You are the advocate for your female, you can't see if she is treated correctly and timely if you aren't there. Likewise, you can't answer immediate treatment questions the veterinary team may have to keep a good pace of treatment.

Though rare nowadays, some vets will allow you to assist in the delivery, mainly if short-staffed. If you are blood shy, you'll probably best in the waiting room.

Discuss with the vet, before any surgery begins:

- Confirm she will be intubated.
- Check that Intravenous fluids will be established to help maintain blood pressure and prevent the effects of blood loss.
- Ask if the choice of anaesthetic drugs will not cross the placental barrier, which can affect the ability of puppies to thrive.
- Suggest absorbable stitches are not used on the skin incision; from my experience, they never dissolved and ended up getting infected.
- Request you are supplied with NSAID painkiller such as Metacam, you may be required to sign a disclaimer.
- Ask that you are provided with a precautionary course of board spectrum antibiotic.

Take with you a towel-covered heated box. For any puppies who may have already been born, and for the puppies born by c-section. Use a heat pad with 12v adaptor for the car or it can be plugged in at the vets. Alternatively, you can use a microwaveable heat pad or a hot water bottle wrapped in a towel.

Post-operation mum should be kept warm and free from stress as she could be confused, tired and in shock. Slowly introduce her to the puppies, but do not leave her unattended until she is content and comfortable around the puppies, which can take many more hours then you think. You can still put the puppies on to feed, while she is sleeping for initial colostrum.

Solo pup protocol

Owners are always surprised when I confirm pregnancy for just one puppy; I'm equally amazed when they comment it's rare.

I've looked over my figures, and at the time of writing there's a 6.4% chance of a pregnancy being a solo puppy, unlike the chances of having a large litter of 10 or more is only 2.3%.

Singleton puppies are not typically a reflection on the sire or dams reproductive capacity, more likely it is due not mating at the most fertile time. Either too early or too late meaning the semen has only just managed to fertilise an egg by surviving and waiting for the egg to mature, or by racing to it super quick before the egg becomes no longer non-viable.

Rumour has it the puppy will be a female if they mated too early and a male puppy if too late.

Should the female be bred from again, ovulation testing should be carried out to prevent the same situation.

The concern regarding small litters is the puppy may be large, due to no competition from siblings for nutrition or space.

This then may cause concern for the delivery and whether the puppy can fit through the pelvis okay, or even if there are enough hormones to trigger contractions and a typical birth.

Once born, there are also concerns about if enough milk will be produced.

I've gathered some of my own data regarding singleton puppies from my clients on the best approach for safe delivery.

- Plan A: 62% of solo puppies were birthed naturally, of which 85% survived.
- Plan B: 100% of solo puppies born by elective c-section survived.
- Plan C: 38% of solo puppies were born by c-section, of which 42% survived.

Plan A: Naturally Whelped

Naturally whelped pups which survived were on average born around 62 days gestation, the survival rate significantly decreased from 63 days onwards.

Owners shared the whelping process was 'typical', confirming the puppy tended to be bigger than average in size.

For some, the labour stages were prolonged and difficult, 15% of the owners who whelped naturally recommended other owners to elective section (Plan B) on the due date. They prefer this choice if in the same situation again.

The majority of owners mentioned no issues with milk production or the need to hand or supplement feed.

25% did visit their vet for additional physical checks and advice. One owner felt they were given poor advice and changed practice during this critical period. Read the Breeder Friendly Vet's chapter, so you aren't in this position, ever.

Plan B is way better than C.

The surviving puppies born by c-section were on average born around 61 days, the survival rate decreased significantly from 65 days.

Some owners expressed they felt their vet had delayed the option of a c-section past 65 days, which compromised the puppy's viability.

The majority of owners who decided to c-section was because their female had shown partial signs of labour then stopped. This suggests second stage inertia due to an oversized puppy and the muscles have become tired trying to expel the puppy.

First stage inertia can also happen with solo babies due to the puppy not stimulating or applying enough pressure on the uterine wall and cervix to trigger a natural birth.

It can be easy to miss primary inertia, so I strongly recommend tracking the dam's temperature before and up to her due date. An additional option is to reverse progesterone test to monitor the decreasing levels, which signify the puppies are ready for birth.

Some puppies were born naturally when the female had been sedated and prepared for surgery. The relaxation of the muscles meant the puppy was easier to pull free; however, these puppies were deceased.

Distressed puppies from difficult delivery did not survive the operation or longer than 2 days after birth. Some seemed weak, and some dams were not attentive to them.

The conclusion is that a singleton puppy can be whelped naturally, the statistics are slightly in their favour.

If the labour is not typical, the chances of c-section increase significantly, but the survival rate also reduces dramatically.

Only a pre-agreed elective c-section (Plan B) increased the survival rate, over being whelped naturally.

The risk can be managed by allowing the female to whelp naturally up to her due date. Should she go more than 1 day over, get an ultrasound scan to check for a foetal heartbeat and if confirmed, opt for an elective section.

Not all puppies can be seen moving or even felt, especially on deep-set breeds, occasionally puppies can be absorbed into the body. If in any doubt have her rescanned to confirm the pregnancy is still viable.

Puppies born two or more days after their due date have significantly less chances of surviving in all whelping methods.

There is a high chance financially that you'll need to cover the costs of a c-section when expecting a solo puppy.

Realistically consider booking an elective c-section (Plan B) with your purpose of a live puppy, while keeping your veterinary cost to a minimum. Planning such events is precisely what's the 7P's are highlighting regarding being a proactive breeder; in doing so will also control your anxiety.

Surviving singleton puppies develop like a typical puppy, into adult dogs. Many commented the puppy ended up larger than the breed standard or their mother.

Solo pups tend to be more demanding when it comes to play and stimulation due to the lack of siblings or playmates, which could have an impact on their social skills and adult behaviour.

To prevent such issues, when possible, allow play with your other dogs to replace sibling interactions. Provide many toys as a source of entertainment and engagement.

Pups can become more dependent on human interaction, and if not well stimulated, can become over-demanding and dominate.

Following a well-structured socialisation program, which we'll talk about in future Chapters will help prevent behavioural issues.

CHAPTER 8

4 Phases of Puppy Progress

I believe you can group the development stages of a litter into four simple phases. Each phase is approximately two weeks long and will take you all the way from newborn to new homes.

- Newborn until 2 weeks of age is the vital phase
- From 2 weeks until 4 weeks being the vetting phase
- From 4 weeks until 6 weeks being the viewings phase
- From 6 weeks until 8 weeks being the venture phase

As a breeder, you'll have numerous actions in each phase, firstly concentrating 'in the whelping box' and over time increasing your key activities to necessary actions 'outside' of the whelping box. Each phase will demand a different skillset from you, and the emphasis will change as you progress through the stages.

This framework puts a structure to the future essential activities which await you, ensuring you don't miss any major milestones.

4 Phases of Puppy Progress			
Period	**Phase**	**Focus** *(approximately)*	**Actions & Activities**
Newborn - 2 wks	1. Vital	100% Within in the whelping box	Newborn checks
			Poorly pups
			Dam checks
2 - 4 wks	2. Vetting	75% Within in the whelping box	Worming
			Weaning
			Socialisation
		25% Outside of the whelping box	Vetting
4 - 6 wks	3. Viewings	50% Within in the whelping box	Toilet training
			Microchipping
		50% Outside of the whelping box	Puppy pen transition
			Viewings
6 - 8 wks	4. Venture	Nearly 100% Outside of the whelping box	Socialisation
			Puppy Info Packs
			Vet check & Vaccs
			Collection

As you can see, there's a fair bit of activity which goes on within the next 8 weeks. Let's take a look in a little more detail.

Phase 1 - Vital : 0 to 2 weeks old

The 'vital' phase starts as soon as the puppies are born and lasts until they are approximately 2 weeks old. You'll initially be focused on the activity 'in' the whelping box.

Namely checking the health of the puppies and dealing with any who fail to thrive. This is also a necessary time to keep a close eye on the mum. She's been through a significant experience and now is the primary provider for the pups.

The first few days after birth, you'll be feeling your feet and getting into a routine, hopefully resulting in contented pups, which are growing well.

Puppy defects

When I was four years old, I remember getting a much wanted and loved doll for Christmas. She wasn't any old doll she was called 'Cricket' and was the first talking doll. She was big for a doll, 25 inches tall with a green pleated skirt and a pink woolly jumper. She effectively had a tape cassette player in her back, and when you played a tape, her eyes and mouth moved.

I loved that doll. However, shortly after her joining the household, she broke. Her mouth stopped moving, and for a short while, I had two Cricket dolls. Yes, spoilt brat alert, I am the youngest and the only girl and I dread to think of what tantrums I went through to get a second one so quickly.

The broken doll was returned to the manufacturer as it was faulty. Sometimes as breeders we get 'faulty' puppies. The problem is these puppies can't be returned to the manufacturer because they aren't a manufactured product, they are the raw result of biology, a living organism.

The science

A puppy's genetic material contains 2.8 billion base pairs of DNA. A 'gene' is a section of DNA which has specific instructions for making a particular molecule. Each puppy has two copies of every gene, one inherited from its mum and one from its dad.

These two genes may be the same, or they may be slightly different. These differing genes contribute to each puppy's unique physical features and account for the differences between each dog and each breed.

Any dog can inherit a faulty gene, and this error and can be passed on in turn to their babies. The gene may have become faulty for many reasons, too many for this book, but the just sheer action of replication can cause an error.

Just like an incorrectly copied recipe, the impact it can have will depend on the type of error made. A spelling mistake of a common ingredient in a recipe may have no effect on the final meal, while the changing of a cooking time could have severe consequences. Similarly, a mutant gene may have no apparent impact, or it could cause a severe health problem.

Congenital abnormalities or birth defects are conditions an animal is born with. Some of these conditions are inherited and tend to occur within particular families or breeds, while others are caused by environmental factors such as chemicals, nutrition or injury during pregnancy. It's often difficult to identify the exact causes.

If the dogs you breed are prone to preventable health conditions, then the necessary health checks, test and supplements should be adhered to in order to reduce the re-occurrence. The attitude as a breeder should be proactive in wanting to breed healthy dogs, this may require testing and screening before breeding, not once a problem has been discovered.

Puppy checks

When a human baby is born, the midwives and doctors will carry out several checks.

Once carried out, the results of tests are given a score out of 10, known as the Apgar score. This score will help decide if the baby needs any immediate treatment during the first moments of life.

This has become a routine procedure since 1953, and the test is carried out at one minute and five minutes old. They check:

- Appearance: skin colour
- Pulse: Heart rate
- Grimace: Reflex response
- Activity: muscle tone
- Respiration: Breathing

Each scored 0, 1 or 2. Babies scoring eight to ten are in excellent condition. Between five and seven are in fair condition and may require airway suction or oxygen. Babies scoring below five maybe be given heat, light and oxygen and a paediatrician may be called for additional help.

So can we apply this to Puppies? Of course!

Puppy checks should apply if the pups were born naturally or by c-section. The newborn checks will have probably been made by the vet if born by c-section; however, do not make any assumptions and ensure they confirm this.

Appearance: Puppies should have bright pink paws and muzzle. They shouldn't be pale or have any blue tint. Each puppy should be checked for abnormalities, including checking all limbs are present and entire, there no open wounds particularly on the skull or tracking the spine. The anus must be present and complete, along with genitalia and the roof of the mouth should be complete with no holes or deep ridges.

Don't be overly concerned about misshapen heads, backwards or twisted rear feet, they will all straighten as the puppy grows. It's usually a product of a lack of development space while growing in the uterus. These are not congenital conditions or defects.

Pulse: A newborn puppy heart rate should be around 200 beats per minute. Typically you can feel their heartbeat when held in the palm of your hand. You can also compare heart rates by holding a puppy in each hand to help identify any untypical faster or slower pulse.

Grimace: Healthy pups should want to nuzzle into your hand with their nose. This is a natural instinct to help them find a teat. Most pups are born hungry and are reasonably loud making puppy squeaking noises which not only informs the Dam of their needs but stimulates her milk production.

Activity: Newborns should be wiggly and active. Never staying still, seeking all corners of the whelping box until content. Pups should not be limp or stretching.

Respiration: Newborn pups normal respiratory rate is around 15-35 breaths per minute. Newborns are typically noisy and mobile. Breathing should not be weak shallow or irregular.

If you notice a puppy not sufficiently meeting the AGAR simple tests, you may need additional intervention from a vet. They may be able to advise you on what's causing the concern and whether it's life-limiting.

In this instance, you will need to make the decision whether to rear any puppies suffering serious conditions, or have them humanely put to sleep.

Pro-life breeders believe all the time the puppy fights, they will fight with them. The problem with this argument is you as the breeder have the foresight and knowledge to know what's ahead, which the puppy doesn't.

This may include future operations required to fix the problem as an adult, lack of insurance coverage because the condition was congenital and present from birth.

The only instance, in my opinion, a puppy should be reared with such life impacting conditions, is because the breeder, that's you, will keep this puppy for its entire life.

No veterinary professional will disagree with the choice of having a puppy with such conditions put to sleep. This will be a decision you will have to make, yep another one, and as a breeder, one you'll live with.

First Feed

Clean mum's teats before initial feeding and when required with salty water. Inverted nipples may be massaged out. The initial first feeds are vital for the puppy's own immune system, as these feeds have a high colostrum level.

One of colostrum's principal function is to pass on mum's antibodies to the puppies. Whatever she has immunity too, her puppies will also. This works because up to 12 hours after birth, the Pups have an 'open gut'. This means they can absorb her antibodies.

This is a time-critical stage, and it's recommended a puppy consumes 5% of their body weight in colostrum within this period.

This is a difficult measurement to make, considering most puppies can lose weight up to three days after birth. Daily weighing will help identify any puppies with rapid or continual weight loss and any potential underlying issues. Think OATH! Observation is key.

Ensure the puppy is correctly 'attached' and suckling, some pups can be slow to latch and mouths may need prying open and teats pushed in. Some 'head nod' too much pushing themselves off, using the back of your hand to prevent this will reduce the habit. If you hear a smacking nose then they puppy is not correctly latched on, good feeding is peaceful and once milk has dropped, even looks easy.

There are products on the market available which are enriched with sources of colostrum to mimic mothers. Typically derived from cows or a complex package of vitamins and essential minerals.

Ideally, the colostrum should come from a source which does not use hormones, pesticides or medications that might concentrate in the colostrum. If possible, always use mum.

Blood plasma is also a source of antibodies which have been used to protect orphaned or ailing puppies. The plasma can be from the dam or even purchased as Frozen Plasma online, supplied by a donor dog.

The plasma can be given orally while the gut is still open and able to absorb the antibodies, typically given three times during the first 36hrs of life.

The plasma also contains vitamin K, which aids blood clotting. It's currently routinely given to newborn human babies in the UK, to prevent a now rare bleeding disorder called haemorrhagic disease.

Puppies should typically feed every 2 to 3 hours. If your puppies are 'free-feeding' in the whelping box with access to mum 24/7, then daily weighing will confirm they are thriving.

If your puppies are in a 'puppy box' and kept separate, then you must ensure they have access to mum frequently and regularly for adequate amounts of time per feed. Approximately 30 minutes for about 12 - 8 times a day.

Puppy Identification

Newborn puppies can be difficult to tell apart, particularly when of similar colours or markings.

Part of being a proactive breeder and following the OATH guidelines is by tracking the progress of each puppy. It's essential you can tell them apart, even more so when 'puppy duties' are being shared in the family or rotated between people.

Whelping collars help quickly to identify each puppy. They can vary in colour, material and quality from ribbon to festival or inpatient hospital-style wristbands or washable and adjustable paracord collars.

You can use your notebook to make a note of each puppy's weight at the same time every day, detailing any observations of general health.

You can download and print for each puppy the free breeder help sheet called 'Puppy Report Card'. This helpsheet and explanatory video in the Home Breeders Hub will help you track the progress of each puppy within a useful and clear template. Visit www.caninefmailyplanner.com/nby to register for the Hub and gain instant access to the vital Breeder Help Sheet.

Mum Checks

I saw a programme about the Seals on the Norfolk coast. Baby seals, also called pups, are totally dependent on their mum, for 3 weeks. After this point, they need to fend for themselves, only 3 weeks to become independent.

During these 3 weeks, they gain up to 2kg a day. That's astounding! Apparently, their mum's milk has around a 60% fat content, which is the equivalent to suckling Mayonnaise.

That said it's vital you feed your mum a high-quality diet, so she can produce good, high-quality milk for her pups. It's said red meat with high-fat content will help milk production, also using a Fenugreek supplement.

She might be consuming up to three her usual amount, with any extra enticing treats or toppers. Females after a c-section may be more reluctant and slower to gain their appetite, so make sure you have some of her favourite easy digestible soft foods ready.

She may pant heavily for a few days after birth, particularly while feeding puppies. This usually is due to her body releasing oxytocin to stimulate her milk production to meet her litter's demand while helping her uterus to contract. You may experience some vaginal discharge at this point, particularly after feeding, this is only a cause for concern if foul-smelling.

The breeder OATH still applies at this stage. Daily checking of temperature is recommended to ensure no initial signs of infection, uterus or mammary. If she has endured a c-section, you should have a course of antibiotics and a painkiller.

Mastitis

Mastitis is an infection which enters the mammary gland via the milk ducts, causing inflammation and a favourable environment for bacteria and the spread of the infection.

If you suspect has mastitis you should seek veterinary advice immediately. Symptoms include hot, sore glands, loss of appetite, depressed or bad odour. She will need antibiotic treatment, warm water compresses and the puppies to continue feeding to empty the mammary glands.

Puppy nails should be kept short by trimming regularly, this is easily done with baby nail clippers as they are soft.

Eclampsia

Eclampsia is an emergency medical condition and life-threatening due to a significant drop in blood calcium levels, which typically occurs in nursing mothers. Eclampsia most commonly occurs when the puppies are one to four weeks of age, and the mother is producing the most milk.

Symptoms can include head tremors, increased body temperature, aggressively panting, restlessness and muscle spasms. This condition can be easily identified with a blood test at your vets and treated quickly.

Every day's a school day

Apparently, the odds of existing as the unique human you are is 400 trillion to 1, that's 400,000,000,000,000 to 1. Certainly insane odds and once born there's the additional luck of where you were born, your health, race and class.

I imagine canine odds to be slightly less, but just as amazing. The fact a puppy has been conceived and born could be classed as a little miracle, but breeding over time will undoubtedly dissolve any complacency.

To coin the phrase "Every day is a School Day" is certainly true. You'll soon learn that not every litter is the same, even though you've nurtured them the same way. Even when following your own 'tried & tested' protocol. Not every puppy will survive in every litter, and it's no reflection of the quality of care you've provided.

Poorly pups

Dogs have extraordinary senses and mum can sometimes sense an unwell puppy before we have realised any symptoms. If mum seems to be disregarding or excluding a puppy, then pay it special attention, she's normally doing this for a reason.

Ensure it's warm, breathing typically, feeding well, gaining weight and sleeping with contentment. A puppy's failure to thrive can be frustrating to deal with, as diagnosing and treatment, might not be and not always successful.

A poorly pup is often cold to touch; if the coat is cold when pressed to your face, they are chilled. The puppies may also be laying limp, crying or unsettled and refusing to nurse. Following the

Breeder OATH guide, you've observed the puppies' unwell' signs and have acknowledged there is an issue.

If a puppy is rejected by its mother, it may be better to remove and isolate, until treatment is successful or there is a noticeable improvement. This moves you into the 'take action' stage of the framework.

Puppy loss is normal and no reflection of the breeder's commitment. It's accepted a possible pre-weaning loss, including stillborn puppies, can be up to 30% of the litter. That's 1 or 2 pups in a litter of 6, typically with about half of these deaths occurring within the first week of life.

Fading puppy syndrome is a term used to describe puppies who are apparently normal at birth, but gradually "fade" and die within the first two weeks of life. It is often too late to save a puppy once symptoms are apparent. There are many factors which contribute to fading puppy syndrome, including:

- Birth defects in the puppy, which may not be immediately apparent.
- Infectious causes.
- Inadequate nursing or milk consumption.
- Low birth weight.
- Lack of milk production or poor quality milk.
- Lack of adequate care from the mother.

Treatment

Always seek veterinary advice for poorly and unwell puppies, in reality, there is a limited amount of treatment which can be offered. Treatments may include all or a combination of:

- A regulated heat source to ensure body temperature is maintained.
- Hand or supplement feeding fluids or milk.
- Re-hydration fluids - oral or injectable.
- Antibiotics - oral fluid or injectable.

- Oxygen supplementation - easing the symptoms but not necessarily fixing the problem.

Hand rearing

Deciding to hand rear should not be taken lightly. Only attempt if prolonged weight loss or other symptoms have been observed. Females milk can take up to 3 days to meet demand; supplement feeding can slow the demand and mean the puppies are missing out on vital colostrum, so don't rush to do this with healthy pups.

No more than 1ml of fluid per 1oz (28g) puppy body weight should be given per feed.

Powdered milk can be purchased at most pet shops, canned evaporated milk can be used as a temporary emergency alternative for not more than 24 hours. Slowly build-up to the ratio of milk and hydration solution such as Liquid Life Aid. Start with 25% milk to 75% hydration mix, to 50:50 to finally 75:25.

There is no right or wrong to picking which feeding method you wish to use, it's a bit like ordering a side to go with your meal at Nando's.

Who's to say the mash isn't better than the peri-salted chips or spicy rice? I recommend you try all methods, when possible and decide.

Sometimes the puppy will prefer a feeding method regardless of your favoured technique, so it's always worth trying all of them.

Always wind the puppy after feeding to reduce the likelihood of Colic. This can be done by elevating the pup's front as if sitting upright and gently rubbing in circular motion its belly on both sides with your thumb and index finger. Infacol can be used if the puppy is prone to discomfort after feeding.

An infant nasal bulb can be useful for all methods of rearing, not just hand-rearing. If a puppy seems to have ingested milk incorrectly, the bulb can be used to help clear the airway.

Bottle Feeding

Bottle feeding is the most traditional way to hand feed. There are all sorts of human and animal bottles with teats which vary in shape and flow. Flat sided, orthodontic teats are not suitable for pups.

Puppies require a full round teat to seal their mouths around, you will also need a slow or adjustable flow teat. If you need to make your own hole, pierce with a pin rather than using scissors. The flow of milk can be slowed by filling the teat with clean sponges and tilting the bottle to restrict milk supply during the feed.

Check you are satisfied with the teat flow rate by dripping on the back of your hand before using. Less is most certainly more in this case.

Royal Canin baby dog milk provides a free bottle and teats ideal for emergencies. I only use the slowest flow with this bottle and have never had any problems.

When first feeding you may need to help seal the puppies mouth around the teat with your free hand, they will soon get the hang of the way to suck. A Puppy can find it confusing to keep switching between mum's teat and a bottle, as the suckling technique is slightly different.

Puppies can become greedy and start to guzzle the milk. Caution must be taken to prevent aspirational pneumonia. This is when fluid is inhaled onto the puppies lungs, and potentially can be life-threatening.

This is one of the main reasons other feeding methods have become so popular, the flow of milk can be controlled better.

Syringe feeding

You are now able to buy nursing syringes which have been modified to include a teat, enabling a puppy to take and latch to the syringe quicker and easier. There are also special long teats available for cleft palate puppies. A quick Google will satisfy your needs.

Sponge feeding

Sponge feeding is another evolution of syringe feeding. It requires a syringe of milk and the small clean wedge-shaped 'make up' sponge.

Methods can vary depending on the puppy, most people dip the small end of the sponge, typically trimmed to fit little mouths forming a teat shape, in milk to get the puppy interested and sucking and then either:

- Insert the syringe into the back of the sponge and fill the sponge cavities with milk, so the puppy can continue sucking the sponge and drawing up more milk.
- Use the syringe to dribble milk down the sponge towards the puppies mouth which they can continue to suck and draw in the milk.

Tube Feeding

As a last resort, you'll need a small feeding tube from your vet or online (size F4 to F7) for newborns and a syringe.

I strongly advise you pre-order and keep this item in a cupboard for emergencies. The puppy should be laying on a flat surface, ready for tubing. Mark out the distance from the point of the nose to the last rib on the tube. This length will reach the stomach, lungs are half this distance. So if the marker is not reached, it is not in the stomach.

Fill the tube with milk removing air bubbles and warm. Slowly feed the tube down, they should seem to swallow it. Stop if pup starts to heave. Then remove smoothly and quickly. This method is most certainly the quickest but also the riskiest. If the tube is incorrectly placed in the lung or the puppy is overfed, the results can be disastrous. However, for puppies in the situation to be tube-fed this could be their only opportunity for survival.

Puppy Loss

> "Have you a dog in Heaven, Lord?
> Is there room for just one more?
> Cause my little dog died today;
> He'll be waiting at your door."
> Anon

The death of a puppy can be painful, especially when you've invested much time and intense energy in aiding them. You may have had to make the decision to have the puppy put to sleep, it may have passed naturally or was even born sleeping.

Puppy death comes at a time when your emotions are typically heightened. You're excited by new life, but are likely to be exhausted. You can feel helpless and disappointed the pup didn't thrive and couldn't be saved.

You will have the option to have the puppy cremated by the vet or home burial.

Home burial may be difficult if you have a 'dog proof' garden that's fully paved or covered in shingle or artificial grass. I have previously had to use a raised flowerbed. This means the hole depth is shallow, which isn't ideal. Once refilled the hole can be covered with a slab, large tile or planter to prevent any other animals discovering.

You may wish to preserve the body of the pup, for your vet to investigate further. Particularly if you are concerned with fading puppy syndrome and are concerned for littermates. If this is the case, you may be required to store the puppy until you can get to the vets.

If necessary deceased puppies can be kept in the freezer, this may initially seem insensitive, but if you wish for post mortem examination, then this is the best method.

Obviously, basic hygiene principles should be adhered to, storing on a bottom shelf, isolated from any food and in numerous plastic bags or a container.

You've probably realised you've invested so much time, energy and effort into these pups and yet they are still only two weeks old. It's understandable why you might put the idea of preparing them for new for their new homes, at the back of your mind. It may seems an age way, but work should begin soon to ensure they find the most suitable owners imaginable. Find out how in the next chapter.

CHAPTER 9

Phase 2 - Vetting : 2 to 4 weeks old

If you want your puppies to go to the best homes, then the vetting process starts during this phase. This means you begin to focus on activities outside of the whelping box, as well as inside. This phase is named after the most challenging activity; new owner vetting.

You will have noticed by now puppies grow at a phenomenal rate and by two weeks old eyes and ears will be opening. This is also the time worming, and eventually, even messier weaning may be introduced.

Why bother with socialisation?

Socialisation is a term often used by dog trainers and in dog books and magazines. What does it actually mean?

Puppies and humans are not born with the social skills they require. The term "socialisation" means the learning process a puppy or child must undergo, to learn key life skills to ensure they are happy and confident in the environment and can communicate effectively within their social group. I'm sure you've seen the Secret Life of a 4 year old, which only highlights the struggle.

We ask a considerable amount from our dogs because not only do they need to understand humans and the human world, they also need to become fluent in their own language of the dog.

Puppies which have been socialised adequately in these early weeks are far less likely to react negatively to new situations, noises, people, dogs and animals. A well-socialised puppy is more likely to integrate quickly, with a new owner, making a more enjoyable and rewarding transition.

One of the major causes of death in dogs under two years old is euthanasia, as a result of behavioural problems. Most of these behaviour problems arise from aggression, nearly always escalated from fear.

Behaviourists and trainers up and down the worldwide are seeing dogs with problems which could easily have been prevented if the first 14 weeks of a dog's life had been appropriately managed.

You can find many 'Puppy Socialisation Check Lists' online, which can be printed and progress tracked, then passed onto the new owners to continue. You must remember exposure alone to the listed items is not socialisation. The puppy, particularly when with their new owners away from littermates will determine if an interaction or experience was positive. No puppy should ever be forced into an interaction.

Some breeds need more socialisation than others, breeds bred to guard or terriers need more, which means starting earlier. It's important for breeders to know how their breed requires, so socialisation can be focused accordingly.

It's also imperative the puppy's new owner continues. The habit when their new puppy comes home. Advice on how to do this should be included in their puppy information pack which I'll cover in later Chapters.

During this book, I merely touch on the subject of socialisation. I mention it because it's the breeder's responsibility to ensure their puppies start on the right path and to educate the new owners. The subject is vast and could be a whole book in itself. If you want to delve more into this world, then check out the highly regarded Puppy Culture Program.

No fear!

The socialisation of a litter can start when the puppies are a few days old during the vital phase. Gentle handling and checking developmental progress are all critical steps in the first few days of a puppy's life.

At 3 weeks old the puppy's eyes are open, while their vision is initially weak, they can see movement.

They also start to hear what is going on around them. They may begin to startle when hearing unexpected sounds but, as their fear response is not fully developed, will quickly return to normal.

This is how they should learn to respond to non-threatening events as an adult, rather than show escalating fear. So all interactions should be positive for the puppy.

The puppies are also starting to learn about the social group. Learning to recognise mother, littermates and humans, this is when the bonding process starts.

You can introduce other animals in the household, dogs and cats as long as they are calm, friendly and vaccinated. People, including kids, begin the bond to humans, ensuring they are handled appropriately. Puppies should be comfortable, upright and in a natural position. This should be done quietly and calmly within the whelping box area.

Stroke the puppies gently with different textured things – woollen glove, a rubber glove, a soft baby's toothbrush – as this will stimulate and develop their sense of touch.

Sound Therapy

Make sure the puppy gets to hear as many sounds as possible. These should include doorbell, TV, doors opening and closing, vacuum cleaner, music, bangs, clatters, conversation, and an introduction to fireworks and thunder. You can buy or stream these noises for the rarer sounds.

These shouldn't be playing all the time and do not need to be loud, but should happen unexpectedly throughout the day at times when the puppies are awake. You are looking for the puppies to notice them and then quickly return to normal.

For most people who rear the puppies in the house with the family, these noises will be nothing new but make sure the puppies get to hear the unexpected ones too.

Provide lots of different things for them to look at, as they are naturally down to new novelties such as toys. Roll objects across their puppy pen and change the light levels. Bounce a sizeable softball outside the pen, roll or drag things past the outside of the pen so the puppy gets used to movement he can't chase. Hang a baby's mobile above the pen for 30 minutes a day (out of reach) for additional stimulation.

The work you put in now as a breeder will most certainly make a tremendous difference to the puppy, and its owners as it grows into adulthood.

Worming

Worming is part of the routine of rearing puppies. Vets will generally advise worming at 2, 4, 6 and 8 weeks. Many breeders have chosen to worm later or less at 3, 5, 7 & 9 or 3, 6 & 9 weeks. You also have the option to worm count. I mentioned this process in the earlier Pregnancy Preparations chapter.

Regular worming, not only protects the puppies but helps prevent the spread of infection and hazardous health risks to other animals and you.

Worm infections carried by your dog do not always display obvious symptoms, so an adequate procedure to identify and treat is essential.

Puppies can appear healthy even when they have worm infections. Signs often include always being hungry but not gaining weight, have a dull coat, have a 'pot-belly' bloated stomach appearance, 'scooting' due to irritated bottom or diarrhoea. You may even see worms being passed in their stools or be vomited if left untreated. Dead worms may be passed in the stools once treatment has been administered.

Drontal and Panacur Paste are typically used to treat worms. Drontal is a one-day treatment, while Panacur is a more comprehensive three-day treatment. Panacur is a broader spectrum treatment which also treats Giardia, another parasitic intestinal infection that generally causes diarrhoea.

Weaning

Weaning can commence when all puppies eyes are open, however, if mum has good milk and the litter size isn't overbearing this doesn't need to be rushed.

The majority of breeds commence weaning around three weeks of age because the puppies will have started growing their teeth, supporting the ability to eat tougher textured foods.

The introduction of weaning food should be a slow transition over the weeks until the puppies are fully weaned at six or seven weeks. Some breeders still allow a daily milk feed until they leave for their new homes if the mother allows; this slow transition reduces the likelihood of engorged teats and mastitis. It's not unusual for mothers to resist wanting to feed the pups or restricting access sooner, which may increase your weaning schedule pace.

Weaning may need to happen at a faster rate if the puppies have been hand-reared, the litter is large or milk production is inadequate. It's acceptable to start weaning puppies once all eyes are open in the litter, this is typically around 10 to 14 days old. Weaning this young can be a bit messier as they may not yet be able to stand steadily and typically more training is required in the behaviour of moving from sucking to licking.

Start weaning by letting the puppies lick a dab of weaning food off the tip of a finger, feeding on a fingertip is similar to them suckling a teat. Once they can stand steadily unsupported, you can tempt them to eat from a shallow bowl or soother Lickimat.

There are many options when weaning, I believe in keeping it simple. Using a transitional food such as a weaning mousse, that's flavoursome and easy to digest and prepare. Add soaked kibble to make a porridge once confidently eating. Over time reduce the mousse and when thoroughly accustomed, make the soaked kibble drier.

Complete raw food feeders can use a weaning paste which is finely ground and super smooth. Over time a transition can be made to a complete puppy raw.

The amount will all depend on your breed and their weight, there's no right or wrong. You want the puppy to have a comfortably full belly, not too full which is hard and uncomfortable. If in doubt, start with less and increase each weaning feeding.

The food will need to eventually increase to be in line with your food manufacture recommendations for age.

Once puppies are competent eaters, they should be fed from individual bowls, reducing the likelihood of developing food guarding or aggression issues.

Putting the feelers out

It's unlikely you'll be able to keep the all the puppies in the litter, so you'll have some available for sale. This is a big responsibility, possibly the biggest as a breeder.

Your choices will have a lifelong impact on the puppy you have bred and raised.

Are there good and bad places to advertise puppies?

I would answer, No.

To me, there are many free online platforms available where you can advertise your litter and find potential new owners for your puppies. These vary in all shapes and formats; if you have a Kennel Club (KC) registered litter, you can advertise through their online chargeable 'Find a Puppy' facility.

You can also use other platforms for pedigree and crossbreeds such as Pets4Homes, Gumtree, Champdogs or free printed papers. You're not allowed to advertise animals on Facebook Marketplace.

There is some snobbery around whether you should be using some of these platforms. Personally, I feel you should use all that's available because you never know how you might find the perfect future puppy owner.

The more important thing is, once you have the enquiries, you do your best to vet these people correctly. You will need a more robust vetting procedure when using some sites, but they have high traffic and more potential enquiries to pick from.

My recommendation is to start advertising as early as possible, once your confident the pups are thriving. Having a multiple-stage vetting process will help you find the genuine enquiries. This will help you to weed out unsuitable potential owners, a bit like Lord Alan Sugar on the TV series, The Apprentice. Your vetting structure should look something like this:

1. Vetting or Questionnaire form
2. Verbal telephone conversation
3. Added to the Waiting list
4. Face to face meeting for puppy viewing

If friends and family have expressed an interest in the litter, then they shouldn't be treated any different in your vetting process. This avoids an 'easy come' easy go ownership attitude. Your primary focus should be to correctly vet people and potential owners, so puppies aren't returned back to you, with additional problems or issues, due to them not investing the time to socialise, care and train them correctly.

By correctly vetting people, you will to reduce, if not eradicate this type of scenario, along with any time wasters.

It's your responsibility to correctly home the puppies you've bred keeping them out of rescue, regardless of their age. There's always strong opinion from anti-breeding activists, with so many dogs ending up in charities or breed rescues. Don't fuel their fire.

Questionnaire / Vetting form

Your vetting form is essentially a questionnaire, which can be built and hosted online if you have some basic computer abilities, or find someone who does. Once it's set up, you can use it for any additional litters you may have. Completed forms can be emailed directly to your inbox and backup's stored online.

Using a vetting form sets the bar of the expectations you expect of any enquiring owners, by them taking the time to complete the form and provide thoughtful answers. Helping you decide if they have qualified as suitable owners, who just aren't looking to purchase a puppy on a whim.

You'll probably receive enquiries through various channels, face to face, email, phone, text, messenger and mobile phone apps. The vetting form is an excellent way of organising your enquiries, all channelled to one place. You can simply respond requesting politely they complete your questionnaire and weblink while providing some necessary information about the litter and available pups.

So what should be on this vetting form?

The purpose is to obtain their basic information and gauge the type of future puppy owner they will be. Questions you may wish to include:

- Personal contact details
- What's their family setup? Kids? Housing type inc. Garden?
- Are they open to home viewings?

- Do they work full time?
- What's their purpose of the puppy? Are they looking for a pet companion, to breed or show the pup?
- Are they looking for a male or female puppy?
- Who will be the primary caregiver?
- Do they currently or have they previously owned dogs? Were they happy with them? Why?
- What do they consider to be an important requirement of the pup?
- Are there any animal allergies in the family?
- Have read the breed standard to understand the breed? The puppies traits?
- What is their ideal training plan?
- What exercise do they think the puppy will need as an adult?
- What is there expectations of a grooming regime?

Your Qualifying Criteria

Vetting really does come down to your own preference and personal criteria, which should be driven by the needs of the puppy. You know the breed behaviours and traits. For example, some breeders will not sell to people who work full time.

Others may not find this an issue if they have provided arrangements such as they work close to home during breaks, family members pet sitting or with dog walkers. They may already have another dog, and this routine has been successful, with no behavioural issues and are now looking for a companion for them.

Declining enquiries

At this stage, you can reject any enquiries which don't meet your satisfaction. Thank them for taking the time to complete the form, confirming there are no puppies available for them at this time.

You have the right to change your mind at any point of the process regardless of how upset the potential owners may become. You notify them of your change of heart by email after a call, or passively just leave them on the waiting list with no puppy allocation. Even if they have viewed and left a deposit, you can return the deposit and explain why you feel they aren't suitable at this time to be allocated a puppy in the litter.

Next stage: Telephone Call

If you are happy with the details they provided, you can contact them and discuss some of their provided answers, helping to form part of the telephone conversation. Question them on some of their responses to drill down more and find out more information, or to explain or educate them.

During this call, you hope to have a frank and honest conversation. You should always go with your gut feeling, intuition is a wonderful thing. If you are happy at this point then, proceed to the next stage, adding them to your waiting list and confirm to them you have done this.

Next stage: Waiting List

It would be great if you had a list of vetted people already waiting once you're female is scanned in pup. This way, you can keep these people engaged and updated with the pregnancy and as the puppies grow and progress.

You won't be able to assign the puppies to an owner until born and thriving, but keeping all on the waiting list updated when born, will ease the process of finding the best candidates.

Don't assume all will want a puppy at the time you have them available. It will depend on timing such as avoiding major life events like weddings, holidays, house moves and career moves combined with their suitability for the litter, depending on available sexes, breed and colours as expressed on their vetting form.

Next Stage: Puppy Viewing

I believe there should be at least one puppy visit before the puppy is sold or collected.

This is an excellent opportunity to be able to meet all of the family, partners and children. Check all the visitors who will be living with the puppy engaged with the pup, and show an interest in their new companion. If they have existing pets, asking to see photos or videos to help you gauge their capability as an owner. Look for:

- If they are in good physical condition? Well-groomed and clean?
- Are they the correct weight? Good muscle definition?
- How well behaved and trained are they?
- Have they shared any problems they've had with them?
- Where is the picture taken, assess the background is it clean and tidy?

If you conduct your viewings before 6 weeks of age, some owners are keen for a second viewing before collection. This can become rather time-consuming. As an alternative, you could host a 'Puppy Party' where all owners attend at one time. You could then educate them in a group setting about future aftercare required and field question which will value the whole group and only have to answer them once!

Deposits

It's standard practice to take a deposit during the first puppy viewing, preventing time wasters, otherwise known as tire kickers or photo collectors. These type of people will be dramatically reduced if you have followed all the four vetting stages.

The deposit should be approximately 10 - 20% of the puppy sale price. The new owners should receive a receipt confirming the amount of deposit, and on which particular puppy.

This puppy preferably should be identifiable by microchip, so there's no confusion or doubt in identifying the pup on collection, especially for the breeds which look the same. Different coloured whelping collars help distinguish the puppies apart visually and easy, particularly for pictures you are sharing with the new owners.

This documentation will potentially save you any future inconvenience. It should clearly state an agreed collection date of the puppy. The puppy must be at least 8 weeks old, the outstanding balance and the method of payment.

If they wish you to run the puppy on for a period past 8 weeks due to their availability or existing commitments. You'll need to consider the puppy's social needs and the time required to continue its socialisation, along with lead and collar training, vaccinations, worming and future toilet training.

You need to consider if you wish to take on this additional role and if there is a cost for the service.

Deciding on a price

Pricing is flexible and is defined by numerous factors. I recommend you look at the prices of similar puppies on the sites you plan to advertise on as a benchmark.

Selling dogs is a simple supply and demand principle. The more desirable your puppies, the easier you can sell, the more you can increase your price. Desirability may be due to the breed itself, popularity and trends, parentage, health screening and even visual appearance; size, coat or eye colours.

Don't be fooled, just because a dog is advertised at a particular price, it doesn't mean that was the price paid.

If you have a waiting list, then you already have a small demand. I would advise of the price range before adding them to your waiting list to ensure serious enquiries.

Some breeders will charge differing fees depending on the individual pup, and how it varies from the littermates, this might be its sex, coat colour etc.

I charge the same fee for all my puppies, as the same effort goes into rearing them, regardless of if one is going to a 'show home' or not I don't feel the 'non-show puppy' is any less quality or should be treated any differently. It's just part of appropriately matching the right puppy to the correct owner's needs.

Puppy age can impact your asking price, once over 10 to 12 weeks, the price can be negatively affected. Pet puppy owners generally want to experience the puppy from the earliest, smallest and 'cutest' age point.

You may find some owners wanting a slightly older puppy who maybe is lead or collar trained, has received full vaccinations and toilet trained. These type of puppies are more convenient for them, not having to fuss with this training.

People who show may prefer to buy a slightly older dog as they are a safer bet. They can see the bone structure and conformation has started to develop. Most breeders are producing puppies for pet owners, their expectations are generally not as finicky and is reflected in the price.

You need to have an awareness of the Animal Welfare Regulations 2018. This came into force 1st October 2018, this is the same act that previously enforced compulsory microchipping and the regulation of tail docking.

Your local authority is responsible for enforcing the legalisation and requirements can vary council to council. You may require a dog breeding license if you breed three litters or more per year or are advertising a business of selling dogs.

The latter is a particular grey area, but they may look at your scale of breeding, range of breeds and frequency of advertising. For home breeders to be considered 'out of scope' for the licence, they should be able to clearly evidence a lack of profit resulting in less than £1,000 which supports you had no 'intent' to make a profit.

The dog breeding licence lower limit is when profits, not income like HMRC (tax office), exceeds £1,000. This would be after you have deducted all your breeding expenses from your puppy sales.

The HMRC currently allow £1,000 income tax-free from trading income, this would include dog breeding sales. Any income over this amount should be declared and included in your annual tax return.

I strongly recommend regardless of if you decide to file a self-assessment, that you keep all your receipts associated with the breeding for at least 7 years. If you are an irregular breeder, I can only foresee issues arising because:

- Past puppy owner has a complaint
- A complaining neighbour with a grudge
- Another breeder who's watchful/jealous/nosey
- Local authorities have received an allegation or following their standard process

A litter of puppies can be 'gifted', so the £1,000 figure is not reached. I personally do not feel any dog should be given for free.

By human nature, we tend not to value or cherish objects we don't pay for. I wouldn't want to encourage a carefree, easy come easy go attitude of any potential owners.

The purchase price of a dog is just the beginning of a long term financial commitment to dog ownership. If they can't afford the purchase price, I would be concerned about ongoing affordability.

Payment methods

Deposits can be taken in cash or cheque as you'll have time to bank and clear before the puppy is collected. Today we now have much faster on the spot payment methods such as mobile banking.

On collection, you should insist on either cash, advanced BACS payment or instant mobile transfer.

Do not accept payments through money transfer companies such as PayPal because they favour the Buyer in any disputes due to their consumer rights. After the puppy is collected, the funds can be 'recalled' without your permission leaving you out of pocket and the puppy unpaid for.

Puppy viewing can be a complete time suck, especially with photo collectors, no shows or last-minute cancellations. If you want to know how to prepare for puppy viewings and how to streamline the process, then the next chapter is for you.

CHAPTER 10

Phase 3 - Viewings : 4 to 6 weeks

I named this phase the 'Viewings' because much of your time will be taken with organising and hosting puppy viewings.

The pups are now between 4 to 6 weeks old and during this phase should be more independent and weaned from their mother. This includes eating solid food and lapping drinking water.

Puppy meals should be 4 to 6 times a day, approximately every 5 hours reducing to 4 meals by 8 weeks old. Mum will begin to get back to her usual self, and her milk should start to dry up due to the puppies suckling less frequently. Meaning her food can also be decreased in proportion size.

Puppy Socialisation

Pups are starting to develop play and problem-solving behaviour. They need challenges, such as toys – things to carry, pull, climb on, move around, tug with littermates. This helps develop strength, coordination, agility and sharing.

Puppies deprived of this can grow up to be poor and slow learners, or as adults, they may become frustrated and develop temperament problems.

Mum may now seem a bit rough with them, at times walking off when they are trying to suckle, growling or even standing on them. This is her way of teaching the puppies how to cope with frustration and learning to overcome it. You can use a t-shirt to cover her undercarriage when weaned or separate her more often.

This is also the time to spend more time with each puppy individually – slowly increasing the time they spend away from their littermates and mother. This will help to prevent separation problems. Developing independence and will encourage bonding with humans helping them manage fear and wariness.

Begin to teach each puppy to get used to being handled by gently restraining them for 3 seconds and then letting go, as long as they are calm and not wriggling.

Build up slowly to 30 seconds, with plenty of praise and reward, so they get used to dealing with the potential frustration of being handled. This is essential for grooming and vet visits, include looking into eyes, ears and mouth.

It's also time to upgrade the whelping box to a puppy playpen by introducing different surfaces. Including a bedding area, play area and toilet area. This may consist of puppy pads (disposable or washable), newspaper, sawdust or shredded t-bags. Vet bed, carpet such as off-cuts or mats, lino, rubber matting will give the puppies lots of different tactile sensations.

Add items the puppies can begin to experiment with - tug toys, Kongs, tunnels, upside-down cardboard boxes with holes cut out, large pieces of vetbed, handle-less bucket or basin on its side, bits of blanket tied at one end to the pen tug and clamber over. They need not be expensive, I've provided a list of ideas in the Breeding on a Budget chapter.

If possible, move the litter around the house giving supervised access to the garden or patio on dry, mild days. This will enable different noises, surfaces, activity levels as part of their ongoing socialisation.

No Likey, No Lighty

I'm assuming you've seen, even in passing, the television programme 'Take me out'. The host Paddy McGuinness helps a male contestant pick from a plethora of ladies. Some have likened it to a 'meat market', others a dating program. I guess times have changed as the Paul O'Grady reboot of 'Blind Date' indeed fell short.

Puppy vetting and viewings are a little bit like dating. Trying to find a lifelong partner they will be happy with for life. In this instance, you the breeder are Paddy, the puppy you are selling is the contestant and the potential owners are all the lovely ladies.

As the host, it's your job to wring dry the ladies of all their secrets and misfortunes by encouraging honesty, and in return 'matching' them to the most suitable contestant, the puppy.

For the 'fit' to be life long, you as the host need to suitably discover interesting and relevant points of the potential owner. This will help that they are correctly matched to the right contestant. This match should be more than just physical appearance (markings or coat colour), but characteristics such as energy level, intelligence and owner commitment.

Do you recall Paddy's catchphrase 'No Likey, No Lighty'?

As they work through various 'rounds', both the females and the male can turn off lights to signify they aren't a suitable match.

It always makes me giggle when the film reel shows the male contestant at the gym and loads turn their lights off assuming he's going to be gym obsessed, food finicky and probably vein. I guess this is what the potential owners have already done when looking and researching other breeds.

This is no different from your puppy vetting and viewing process. By asking questions to find out if what they put in their questionnaire is true? If you get the feeling they aren't suitable, turn your light off and start again looking for a better suitor, or move to the next person on your waiting list.

Viewings allow the new owners to acquaint themselves with their puppy and you. Selection of puppy and owner pairings should if possible be decided, or at least only a selection of two puppies, not the whole litter. Like the final round of the dating programme, this streamlining of choice will help keep the viewing to a reasonable time and with purpose.

Explain to the owners why you consider the puppy suggested as the best match for them — suiting their lifestyle and the puppies personality and characteristics. A litter where their parents are of the same breed will still have a variety of characteristics.

- **Active and lively puppies** are suitable for busy, large, young families or owners who are physically active.
- **Intelligent and inquisitive pups** may better be suited to owners who have an interest in training the dog or canine activities such as obedience, agility, scent work, flyball etc.
- **Calm and laid back puppies** may be better suited to a mature household, where the pace of life is slower and therefore less stressful, but companionship is consistent and frequent.

The larger the litter, the more puppies, the more potential owners, so the more difficult the logistics of arranging viewings. This is where a Puppy Party might be beneficial for optional second viewings.

As a breeder, it is good to be flexible but were possible, scheduled viewings around the puppies ' regular' play hours. This will ensure the potential owners see the pups at their best, displaying their true temperament and energy levels.

Try to keep viewings to 60 mins and no more than 90. Inform the potential owners you've allocated a visitor slot to prevent late arrivals, cancellations and overrunning. Find out who will be attending, or state who you wish to attend.

Some visitors may see this as a day out for the whole family, a bit like a petting zoo and may never really have a serious interest in securing a puppy. You need to ensure your vetting process avoids these type of people.

My preference is to hold viewings at 6 weeks of age over a weekend, you'll struggle to fit four in a day, if not correctly scheduled. Express to the visitors the importance of being on time and lateness will only result in a shorter viewing slot.

I personally don't allow viewings at a younger age for security, most puppies aren't microchipped until 6 wks of age. It's advantageous the puppies are chipped before viewings, benefits as to why later in this book.

Be considerate, some dam's may become anxious when her puppies are being handled by strangers.

Potential owners can become demanding, mainly due to their excitement; it's your responsibility to set their expectations.

You may need to explain that you still have other responsibilities such as your other dogs to care for, family, work and any other commitments which might prevent you from providing constant updates.

Your life will be easier if you set up some form of group chat for all owners. This way you can post litter pictures to all and they can pick out their own puppy from the images and answer each other's questions, or you can respond to all quicker than on a 1 to 1 basis.

During this phase, it's also good to provide a 'shopping list' of items they will need to purchase for their puppy, including bedding, crate, food, toys, puppy pads, first aid kit, any breed-specific items and grooming products.

Puppy Protection

I've got to admit I'm not a massive fan of horror movies, I much prefer a thriller. I always watch horror films thinking, 'jeez you're giving a ton of unstable people, some really good and scary ideas.

I'm a really jumpy person, even if someone comes into a room unannounced, I'm usually so focused on a task I leap out my skin with surprise. Me and horror movies at the cinema with popcorn is never a good idea.

This was taken to another level when I was a participant of Thorpe Park's SAW Live Horror Maze. There was no way I was going in first, leading the 'chain' of people through the maze. I was more than happy to be well and truly wedged in the middle of the pack, safely surrounded by people.

As soon as we walked into serial killers Jigsaw's lair, my stomach was in knots. I was no longer in control, the anticipation of the unknown was unbearable. I was at his mercy.

The good thing about this maze was it wasn't real, all the characters are actors, and after being submerged in 20 minutes of hell. I exited through the gift shop into daylight and fresh air, which was cherished at the moment.

I frequently see horrific news, to me it feels like I was in my own horror movie. This would instantly bring back the same emotions, more intense because it was real.

It's believed around 2,000 stolen dogs are reported per year, and the number just keeps increasing.

"Dog breeder offers £50,000 reward for her 11 puppies that were stolen by a gang of thugs armed with knives.

The three raiders, that pretended to be gas men, burst into Victoria Orley's property while her son, 16, and daughter, 13, were alone"

THE SUN - OCT'18

Just seeing social posts about missing animals, makes my stomach flip with concern. For many of us, our dogs are one of the most precious things in the world.

As breeders and owners, it's imperative you keep your dogs protected and safe. Dogs have become highly desirable, and over recent years dog theft has significantly increased. Mainly driven by the fluctuation of the monetary value of animals. A Belgium racing pigeon called 'Armando' recently sold for £1.1mil to some Chinese bird fancier's, I think this proves my case.

It's easier to steal and distribute a litter of puppies, then adults who are easier to identify and more likely to defend themselves.

Microchipping is one of the most effective ways of reuniting dogs with their owners, as long as the contact details are current.

Breeders can be at extreme risk when selling puppies, typically if litters aren't chipped and puppy viewings have started. This is an area of risk you need to manage. Completing the four vetting stages will help deter any possible undesirables, but it's not foolproof.

Puppy viewings involve you allowing relatively unknown strangers into your home, which could potentially leave you a victim of crime.

Don't provide your exact address, until 24-48hrs before the viewing. Your vetting process should have meant you have the visitors full contact details, including address and contact numbers.

Explain to them you have safeguarding procedures which will be carried out before any puppies are viewed and regardless of if they decide to purchase a puppy.

Request the visitors provide identification in advance, copies of identification, e.g. Passport or Photographic Driving Licence with a utility bill, registered at the same address.

This is quickly done by taking a picture using their mobile phone and forwarding the image with apps such as Whatsapp, Messenger or email.

You can also request they bring the originals on their visit, so you can check they haven't been edited or counterfeited.

I have known breeders to also take note of the visitor's cars registration during their visit.

Consider how much of your house the visitors will see. Possible criminals' acting' interested in viewing a litter, could be 'casing your premises' to return uninvited later.

- Will they see all your dogs and where they are housed?
- What about the layout of the house and garden security?
- Can they see where your back door is located?
- Is the neighbourhood built-up, how far away are your neighbours?
- Did you tell them in conversation about your availability or when the house is unoccupied?
- Or even who else lives at the premises?

Never have visitors when you are the only person on the premises. Two strangers could soon dominate a situation, and you'll have no help or immediate backup.

Consider investing in a security system to protect you, your house and your dogs. There are many types of surveillance systems, and it's worth seeking professional advice due to the vast array of options.

Always have your and your dog's safety and protection at the forefront of your mind. Treat every visitor with vigilance to prevent becoming part of ever-increasing the 'dog theft' statics, particularly if you breed high-value puppies.

The importance of chipping

Since April 2016, it's your responsibility as a breeder to ensure the puppies you breed are microchipped, before they leave for their new homes. There is no minimum age for microchipping. However, most microchip implanters are trained generally to chip at six weeks of age, because this is when most puppies are of a suitable size.

So what are your options as a breeder?

You have the choice of having the puppy microchipped at the vet's, having a mobile implanter or microchipper, or learning to chip your own puppies.

Depending on the frequency of breeding and your fear, or not, of needles and inflicting minor pain. You may decide to learn to microchip your own puppies, this is rarely the cheapest option as to receive a discounted and competitive price with microchips typically requires a large bulk purchase. Generally in the range of 100, along with the mandatory correct disposal of the needles, plus the training itself. For many breeders, this generally isn't a cost-effective option.

Another option is to have the puppy microchipped at the vets. This is sometimes favourable if the vet is offering a puppy package, where it includes a health check, wormer and first vaccinations.

If you decide not to opt for selling a pre-vaccinated puppy, then another choice or alternative would be to use a mobile implanter. The implanter should be insured and trained for such activities and services, using chips registered to a national database.

This service saves you the inconvenience of moving puppies, particularly large puppies or large litters, from your home to a veterinary practice. Whereby their nature accommodates unwell, sick, and injured animals, which is not an ideal place to be taking young puppies.

Having your puppies microchipped at home means they don't have a negative initial first experience at the vet, which also supports their positive socialisation programme.

You'll find puppies microchipped at home generally, are underwhelmed by the experience. They don't find it stressful because they're in their natural home environment. Even after a sharp needle, they generally recover quickly and get back to play with their siblings or sleep.

Microchips come in numerous sizes the most popular sizes being standard which is 12 mm in length and the mini, which is 8mm. The shorter the chip means they are also fractionally narrower, along with the needle. A standard chip is generally suitable for any medium to giant-sized breed.

You may opt for a mini chip for any small or toy breeds or generally dogs who don't really have much scruff around the neck. The implanter will advise you if the chip of your choice is not suitable.

The audit of a microchip must legally go from implanter to breeder and breeder to new owner. No implanter will be able to transfer the chip directly to the new owners. There has to be a clear audit trail.

It's worth asking when you're enquiring about the cost of microchipping, whether there are additional charges to transfer the pup from breeder to new owner. There are a small number of chip suppliers which offer this service for free, but the majority do not.

It's the new owner's responsibility, to ensure they are the registered keepers on the puppies microchip details. Some chip suppliers provide a 'Breeder Account' to initiate the transfer.

I generally advise breeders not to rush the transfer of ownership from breeder to the owner, until the puppy has been taken for their own vet for an independent health check and have passed with satisfaction.

I suggest the transfer should be made at this point. If the transfer is made before and for whatever reason, the puppy is returned, there may be additional costs in the transferring back to the breeder or the following new owner.

If you have a breed who look similar, such as Labradors, Rottweiler etc., you really need to be able to identify between the puppies for viewings. You can use coloured whelping I.D collars or markings on their body with nail varnish or Tipp-Ex, or even shave small parts of the coat.

If the puppies keep taking the collars off or the marking isn't staying on, then I strongly recommend you buy your own micro-chip scanner.

These are typically picked up online for a low price, there are newer versions of scanners being developed which plug into your mobile phones, so you no longer need batteries or USB charging.

If you are in two minds as to whether you should sell your puppies vaccinated, and unsure what additional support and information you are expected to provide puppy owners, then don't skip the next chapter.

CHAPTER 11

Phase 4 - Venture : 6 to 8 weeks old

The final phase of Puppy progress is called Venture, because during this phase puppies venture outside the home, possibly as part of their socialisation schedule, trips to the vets or the finale when they are collected by their new owners.

Week 5 to 7 is when the pups are curious. These weeks are a crucial time for the Puppy's brain development. This is when puppies are at their most curious and willing to approach people. At the same time, their natural fearfulness starts to grow being shaped by their environment. Hazard avoidance typically begins around 49 days old (7 weeks).

Spending time with the puppies encouraging them to follow you, playing with them, making eye contact while stroking and handling is great. Continue to pick them up safely and holding getting them used to enjoying human contact. Make sure all these interactions are favourable for the Puppy.

Being exposed to different types of people – women, men, children, people with beards, hats, high heels, hoods etc. – and they have positive and rewarding experiences to associate with them such as praise, treats and fun games.

Put more interactive toys into the puppy pen, include wobbly objects, tunnels, suspended tennis balls. Larger balls which can be rolled about, empty plastic bottles with some dry pasta in, trays filled with stones or shallow water, raised beds and low platforms such as shallow steps.

As they are now eating solid foods, feed them individually from different bowl sizes and shapes, plastic or metal and from your hand.

This is the time to teach the puppies to get used to wearing a light collar – only for a few minutes a day while they are thinking about other things, building it up over the next couple of weeks. Do not leave collars on when they are in a crate or playpen, or when unsupervised.

If you have used Puppy Whelping collars, then they will be used to this, but you may wish to extend further by upgrading to a puppy training collar and attaching a lead.

You can share photos with the new owners of their Puppy participating in the socialisation, with structured interactions and experiences to demonstrate all the work which has been done with their Puppy.

Vet & Vaccinations

Taking your litter to the vet is an ideal opportunity to take the puppies out in the car, as part of their socialisation. Alternatively just driving around the block, seeing and smelling things which will be part of their daily life, including passing traffic, bikes and buses. This can be done while parking the car and having the boot open with pups secured with a crate or cage while traffic passes slowly, no faster than 20-30mph.

Some breeders do not get their puppies vaccinated before leaving, and there's a good argument for this. Firstly, vaccinating puppies from a too young age, when they already have immunity from their mother can be considered as counterproductive.

"The WSAVA (World Small Animal Veterinary Association) states the last puppy vaccine against the core diseases should be given at 14-16 weeks of age. This is because, before this time, the mother passes immunity to her puppies, and this 'maternal immunity' can prevent the vaccine from working".

Vaccinating puppies at eight weeks is generally too early. Still, many breeders do this for convenience for the new owners and to demonstrate their consideration for the puppies long term health.

Another potential problem is that puppies already vaccinated if the new owner's vet does not store the same batch and brand of vaccination. They will be forced to restart the inoculations.

This will result in the puppy being over-inoculated, meaning a lot of chemicals to be injected into a puppy who's still rapidly developing and growing.

Plus breeders like and want the new owners to have made an effort to find a suitable vet. Ensuring they have their own independent health check, which may be stated in your sales contract and impact your return policy.

Puppy Collection

I always get asked 'Do you get upset or cry when the pups leave?'

My answer is ALWAYS 'No.'.

When you put the puppy owners through such a robust vetting process, you know you've found five-star homes. The puppies are a the point where they have a considerable demand for socialisation, new structured interactions, experiences and entertainment.

The collection is the final round of 'Take me out', the picking is already done. The trip to Fernando's for the first date is equal to the pup leaving for their next adventure.

On collection day it's best to schedule times slots similar to your initial viewings, to prevent clashes if you have people collecting on the same day. There are two key things which are vital, and must be given to the new owner when it comes to collection time:

- The puppy
- A puppy information pack

The Puppy

It's advisable to request puppies are collected early in the morning, this will ensure they have the full day to settle into their new environment. Ultimately this full-day introduction to their new home should result in a peaceful first night sleep for the new owners.

Puppies should not be fed a least two hours before collection and provide a reduced meal size if they have a long journey, of over an hour.

The puppy should be in good health; if you are in any doubt, then you must seek veterinary advice. It's not fair on the new owner or the puppy to let them go to a new home, only to deteriorate in health, even if it means holding the puppy back.

New environments and a change of water can be enough to unsettle the most robust of puppies. If you have any doubt to the long term health of the puppy, this puppy must not be sold until you've received veterinary advice on how this will impact the puppy as it grows and the future medical care it may need.

There are no major concerns with selling puppies with diagnosed ailments, as long as the owners are aware of the condition, and it is noted in the sale contract.

For instance, it's not uncommon for hernias or low-grade heart murmurs to be discovered. Neither of these may need operating, but a responsible breeder would discount the puppy sale price. This discount, if the owner were unable to insure the condition, would enable the owner to be able to afford the initial treatment.

If a puppy had received a procedure before collection, the owner should be informed. This might include treatments such as tail docking, declawing or cherry eye removal.

Hereditary conditions may impact the owner's decision to continue with the purchase of the puppy, particularly if they wanted the dog for a specific reason such as for breeding or to exhibit.

Every breeder should be responsible for the puppies they breed, should you experience such situations then you must be willing to keep the puppy until the most suitable home is found.

Your ideal plan to have the entire litter homed by 8 weeks old may not be a reality.

The Puppy Information Pack

For most adults collecting a puppy is the closet they get to rekindling their memories as a child on Christmas morning. This exciting experience means much of what you say at collection will be forgotten.

For this reason, I wouldn't overload them with information at this point, but instead, supply them with a Puppy Information Pack. This is the ideal resource for them to refer to once the dust settles, a bit like a user manual to a new Christmas present or cooking instructions for a ready meal.

What should be in the Puppy Information Pack?

Puppy Information Packs are also called Puppy Packs and should be provided by all breeders of puppies whether pedigree, cross or mixed bred. The packs can come in all shapes and sizes. Many are elaborate and creative; whatever yours may look like there are some essential items it should include:

- Sales Contract
- Worming regime
- Microchip number and documents
- Puppy Pet Insurance details
- Feeding advice including a Diet Sheet
- Registration details (if any) including copies of relevant health certificates, e.g. DNA
- Parentage information including copies of health certificates
- Vaccination certificate(if any)
- Information:

- o Toilet training
- o ExerciseTraining
- o Grooming
- o Socialisation

Let's look at the essential items individually.

Sales Contract

A sales contract will ensure the transaction is understood by both parties, providing clarity and avoiding any ambiguity during the sales process. Failure to do this could potentially result in a disagreement between you and the puppy owner, which ultimately could result in court action. Have you seen the number of puppy cases featured on TV shows like Judge Rinder?

The contract should make clear what type of breeder you are, the majority of Home Breeders are private breeders and do not hold a dog breeding license.

Licenced dog breeders may potentially be considered breeding for profit, meaning they are considered a commercial breeder and may have to abide by The Consumer Rights Act 2015. This act gives purchasers, the puppy owners, entitlements to return or reject the goods 'the puppy'. You may need to seek additional advice and clarity from your local authority and Citizen Advice if you have a Dog Breeder License.

The contract should identify the puppy with a description and microchip number, along with parents details, date of birth, current health status and acknowledge any known conditions.

It should as a contract, provide the address of both parties, the breeder and puppy owner, plus signed and dated by all. Both parties should keep a copy of this document for their records.

Provide a copy of the sales contract in advance of collection, so the owners have an opportunity to read it through thoroughly and ask any questions.

Worming regime

The puppies should have been wormed routinely, or worm counted while in your care. This should be documented in the puppies information pack, so the new owners can continue the treatment. They need to know:

- When the puppy was last wormed
- Product used
- When next worming is due
- Current weight

It should be explained routine worming or count not only protects the puppy but helps to prevent the spread of infection and potentially hazardous health risks to other animals and humans.

Puppy's microchip number

You should provide the new owner with the puppies microchip number and process of how the transfer from you to them will be initiated.

It's the owner's responsibility to ensure the puppies contact details are correct and up-to-date.

Puppy Pet Insurance

You will be required to activate the puppy's free insurance around the collection date, and include the cover certificate in their pack. You must pre-register with such schemes, so organise in advance of litter arrival. These schemes are of no cost to you.

Insurance will only cover puppies from 8 weeks of age as part of the Breeder Charter and Kennel Club's Code of Ethics. The insurance may be nulled if this requirement is not met.

Feeding advice

You need to explain to the new owners the importance of feeding the Puppy correctly for their health, development and general wellbeing.

At 8 weeks, the Puppy should be on 4 meals a day, little and often not to overstretch their stomach. Food should not be left down, so they can 'free graze'. Any uneaten food after 20 minutes should be disregarded.

By the time a puppy reaches 14 weeks, they will need roughly the same amount as when they are an adult. Remind the owners the bowl size will need to increase as the Puppy grows.

The quantity of food per meal should increase when the number of meals reduces, they should always have water available for the Puppy.

Some breeders do provide a bottle of tap water, to help reduce any chances of stomach upset, especially if the Puppy is going to live in an area of significantly differing water type or quality.

The new owners shouldn't initially change the Puppy's food, as this could cause havoc with their digestion and toilet training regime. You'll need to provide the new owners with information on:

- **Your Puppy's Current Diet**
- **Number of Meals (per day)& current meal times**
- **Type of Food (supply a sample)**
- **Quantity (daily/per meal)**

Remind the owners not to feed the Puppy an hour before or after exercise or play, as this could lead to stomach dilation and torsion. This is also known as Bloat, which is a life-threatening condition requiring immediate veterinary intervention.

If the Puppy you bred, as a breed is susceptible to this condition. Then provide advice on additional precautionary measures or ensure they ask their vet for further information.

Slippery elm is an animal safe tree bark product, which soothes gastrointestinal inflammation or irritation. It can be easily sprinkled on food and consumed. It's a useful product should a puppy have a loose tum. If the problems persist, for more then 24 hours, then they must be taken to the vet to be checked for more serious illnesses.

Treats

Giving treats is an excellent way to reward the Puppy during training, and encourage the behaviours the new owners want.

There are a wide variety of prepared and natural treats on the market which vary hugely in quality. Some commercial treats have lots of sugar, colourings, milk products and fat in them, so the label should always be checked.

Measuring the Puppy's meal kibble will prevent overfeeding and obesity and can be used during training. This will help the Puppy keep a calorie-controlled diet and avoid unnecessary weight gain.

Your packs should include items which new owners can familiarise themselves with, understanding what things are toxic or poisonous to dogs and dangerous products to avoid, like cowhide chews.

Toxic & Poisonous

- Alcohol
- Chocolate
- Coffee/Caffeine
- Grapes/Raisins/Currants/Sultanas
- Artificial sweeteners containing xylitol
- Some human vitamins and supplements
- Mouldy food

- Onions, chives and garlic
- Slug pellets and other pesticides
- Yeast/Dough
- Some garden/household plants
- Macadamia nuts
- Brassica plants (cabbage, broccoli, cauliflower, swede, turnip)

Registration details

If your puppies are Kennel Club registered, you agree to abide the Kennel Club Code of Ethics. One of the points states:

"Will ensure that all relevant Kennel Club documents are provided to the new owner when selling or transferring a dog, and will agree, in writing, to forward any relevant documents at the earliest opportunity, if not immediately available."

I recommend you register your litter no later than 6 weeks of age, to ensure you receive the paperwork to pass to the new owners.

Owners should be provided with the 'Transfer of Ownership' registration form, and the minimum of a 5 generation pedigree.

If the puppy is crossbred breeders have been known to provide an informal 'Birth Certificate' to recognise the special event, free templates can be found with Google.

Any copies of the parents and puppies official health certificates should be included.

Parentage Information

If the puppy is a pedigree breed, then examples of a breed's specific traits, features and characteristics should be provided. These can be found on the Kennel Club website under 'breed standard' or via Breed clubs.

If the puppy is mixed or crossbred, the pack should contain information about both parents breeds, or what seems to be the most dominant features and characteristics.

This information should be a general overview, including:

- **Adult size**
- **Adult weight**
- **Temperament**
- **Energy levels**
- **Exercise requirements**
- **Grooming needs**

Any other relevant information, e.g. copies of their health certificates.

Vaccination Certificate

There are a number of common life-threatening infectious diseases, which dogs are susceptible to throughout their life. Vaccines are the most effective way to prevent these diseases, as they teach the immune system how to create antibodies protecting them from diseases.

It's widely accepted the core vaccines for dogs to protect against Canine Distemper, Hepatitis, Parvovirus. Plus non-core vaccines are also available and should be administered depending on the dog's lifestyle and geographic location, these include Leptospirosis and Kennel Cough.

If you do decide to sell puppies already vaccinated, you need to provide the owners with:

- **What vaccinations they've received**
- **Date administered**
- **When any additional vaccinations are required to complete the course**

Typically these details are in the vaccination certificate the vet provides, also detailing the products used. This should be passed onto the new owners to continue the course, and use as evidence for future boarding kennels and dog training classes.

In the current climate, breeders are starting to question the effectiveness of vaccinating puppies under 14 weeks of age. There are concerns about the adverse reactions, including death, due to having Lepto 4. Not all brands are the same and reaction to vaccines are mainly related to the vehicle used to resuspend them.

It changes with every brand, so it is vital to check these details if you have concerns. Some breeders are opting to use Lepto 2, rather then Lepto 4.

It's worth asking your vet practice, what they routinely prescribe and request your preference. If they are unable to meet your request, you may need to find an alternative practice who is able too. Please check back to the whole Chapter I wrote on the importance of finding the vet rights for you.

There are also some long term concerns about annual 'Booster' protocol offered by vets. Some owners have taken to titre blood testing, this is a simple blood test which can detect if your dog has antibodies to a disease, and to what degree. Identifying this information, the vet can advise owners if re-vaccination is even required.

You may wish to talk to your preferred vet, about this being an option being available for your older dogs. I have seen vets offer conventional and holistic monthly care plans, incorporating these newer practices and approaches to vaccinating. You can carry out your own additional research through of the World Small Animal Veterinary Association (WSAVA) website and read their Guidelines for the Vaccination of Dogs and Cats.

Toilet Training

Lack of basic toilet training and the struggles, for the new owner, is enough to send them into a cycle of despair and possibly start regretting their puppy purchase.

If you have trained your puppies using pads, shredded bales or even outside then make sure you pass your current toilet regime to the new owners.

There will be accidents, and you should prepare the owners for this. However, they will need to create their own daily routine by establishing a place in the garden for the puppy to toilet and have the puppy visit it frequently.

Remind the owners like babies, puppies have poor bladder control and need to go to the toilet several times an hour when they are awake. They will usually need to be taken outside first thing in the morning, last thing at night, after each meal, waking from a nap, and after any exercise, play or excitement.

A specific cue word or phrase should be used when the puppy is actually going to the toilet, so the puppy will associate the word with the action and should learn to go on command and be praised for any successful efforts. Remind the owners, patience and consistency is key.

Exercise information

Exercise is essential not only for fitness but also for mental stimulation. Puppies need much less exercise than fully-grown dogs. A good rule of thumb is a ratio of five minutes of exercise per month of age (up to twice a day) until the puppy is fully grown.

A puppy would have completed their vaccinations by the earliest 12 weeks of age, at this point as a guide they would require no more than 15 minutes. At four months then 20 minutes and so on. Advise the new owners approximately:

The number of walks and Duration of exercise required for the page of the puppy at:

- 3-4 months
- 4-6 months
- 6-9 months
- 9-12 months
- 1 year +

Remind the owners about Bloat which I've covered in the Feeding advice section.

Training information

"Hyt ys old Englysch sawe: A mayde schuld be seen, but not herd."

John Mirk, circa 1450

Today this would be understood as 'Children should be seen and not heard', meaning children were allowed to be present during a conversation, but should not speak unless they are spoken to.

This was seen as good parenting, resulting in well-manned children. Manners are still highly regarded today and are a reflection of outstanding parenting.

It's really no different with dogs. Your new owners will be observed by other dog owners, friends, family and joe public at how well they achieve 'Puppy Parent' status.

It might not come naturally to them, and the puppy might not either. So receiving or attending some basic dog training will go a long way, will help them to strive for a well-adjusted dog and trusted relationship.

Every puppy should be taught good manners and have valuable lessons in basic control and social interaction. Remember these puppies are living in two worlds, human and canine. Basic training should include:

- Responding to their name.
- Learning how to greet and behave politely around other people and dogs.
- To come back when called.
- To walk nicely on the lead.
- To sit down and stay on command.
- To allow grooming and examination by you or any pet professional.

Many dog trainers offer puppy introduction workshops to ensure both owner and puppy to start on the right path to success. There are lots of schools of thought on dog training, and it is naturally important they find a class and training instructors with the right approach for them and the puppy.

A good place start is the Association of Pet Dog Trainers (www.apdt.co.uk) or Animal Behaviour & Training Council (www.abtcouncil.org.uk). Both whose members have all been formally assessed based on qualifications, experience and knowledge and who are all force-free, reward-based trainers.

Grooming information

The Basics

You've started the basics of 'touch' with your socialisation programme, to aid the dogs future grooming regime. This learning relationship must continue with the new owners; sessions should be kept short, increasing over time. The experience should always be positive, reward with praise and suitable treats.

Any struggling should be handled firmly but kindly if the Puppy is frustrated, mischievous or even afraid. Weekly grooming enables checks for cleanliness, overall health including checking for parasites such as fleas and ticks and any suspicious lumps and bumps.

A puppy's ears should be checked to see if they are clean. Excess dirt can be removed from the inside of the ear flap with clean and damp cotton wool to eliminate wax. Never probe inside the ear. Any odour is usually a sign of infection, and the Puppy should be taken to a vet.

Eyes should be kept clean; if tear staining is constant and excessive, the eye should be checked for conditions. There may be health issues causing this, such as incorrect eyelids and lashes.

Nail trimming can be dramatic for some puppies as they develop into adults. They almost react like some kids when they are getting their first hair cut. Time spent on this as a puppy will undoubtedly benefit the owner in the long term and start before they enter the fear phase.

If nails become excessively long, the tip of the claw can be removed with nail clippers as a puppy. Developing to guillotine clippers or powered nail grinders. Care should be taken not to cut the quick, which can be tricky on dark nails. Walking on pavements will help naturally file nails down during exercise.

External Parasites

A parasite is something which lives on another animal and gets its nourishment from them. If left unchecked, the parasite causes disease or even death. The most common external parasites found on dogs are fleas and ticks. These are treatable and preventable.

Coat Types

A dog's coat generally takes the majority of the grooming time. They come in five different types; it should be explained to the new owners what coat their Puppy has, and what grooming it will require.

The 5 categories of coat type:

1. **Wool coats** – Dense, bouncy coat requiring great care. A coat of high maintenance which requires specific drying techniques and trimming styles. Requires approximately 40 minutes twice a week, to prevent mats and tangles forming.
2. **Double coats** – Dense coat with soft undercoat concealed by a long topcoat, requiring approximately 30-40 minutes once a week.
3. **Silky Coats** – Silky texture not necessarily with coat length requires approximately 20-40 minutes a week.
4. **Wire coats** – Coarse, harsh topcoat with a soft undercoat, requiring approximately 30 minutes once a week to prevent mats and tangles forming.
5. **Smooth Coats** – Short and tight to the body, low maintenance. Grooming achieved by removing the dead coat to leave a glossy finish requires, approximately 10 minutes once a week to prevent heavy shedding.

Factors like neutering, age, poor diet and poor health can dramatically influence a dog's coat. Your Puppy pack should include the Puppy's grooming requirements explaining:

- Coat Type(e.g. wire, double)
- Amount of Grooming Required a week
- Suggested Grooming Equipment, e.g. types of brushes

Professional grooming

Some breeds may benefit professional trimming and styling. Owners who lead busy lifestyles, and can't commit to the time or feel they don't have the skillset will need to use a Groomer regularly.

Most coated breeds will require full grooming once every four to six weeks, even short-coated breeds can benefit from a 'wash and brush' to remove dust and dirt.

Well, respected groomers will have a waiting list, you should advise the owners to find a suitable groomer before collecting their Puppy as initial interaction can form part of their socialisation.

Socialisation information

You've done an excellent job so far by correctly socialising the puppy, and this needs to continue with their new owner. Puppies meaningful learning and development window closes around 14 weeks of age which coincides with their vaccinations.

Ensure the owners are aware exercise isn't crucial at this point as the puppy joints and muscles are still developing and could be damaged. Walks aren't the same as socialising. A puppy can still get used to everyday life, without excessive exercise.

If possible, ensure structured interaction and experiences in a safe environment, where there is no risk and the puppy. They can mix with vaccinated animals and people in a private garden.

You may be able to recommend books for them to read or local trainers who can help them during this vital period. Rather than them relying on generic vet advice to typically attend puppy parties.

Caution should be taken during these parties, ensuring they are well supervised. Poor management could fuel anti-social behaviour, from the overplay or mismatched puppies. Overexcited or boisterous puppies potentially biting, making the experience extremely detrimental for your puppy. Rather than supporting the plan to sculpt a well-balanced and friendly dog.

Additional Extras

If this wasn't enough, Breeders have been known, and seemingly enjoy building and providing packs with a plethora of additional extras, not limited to:

- Puppy pacifier/toy

- Bedding
- Treats
- Bowl
- Collar & Lead
- Grooming starter kit
- First aid kit
- Cage/crate

The list is pretty explanatory, except maybe the Puppy pacifier. This can be a simple as an unwashed toy, or Puppy bedding, if vetbed, cut into pieces to be used as a comforter to help the puppy's during their first view nights in their new home as part of their puppy pack.

I've seen extremely well-considered themed information packs, and this is only limited by your own creativity. 'It's a boy or girl' balloons tied to bags which have all the relevant information. McDonald's 'Happy Meal' themed or puppies leaving with their 'First Day at School' rucksacks.

This kind of thing is not essential, obviously the puppy is the most important thing. It does suggest symbolisation of the thoughtfulness and care which has gone into rearing the litter when this amount of time and effort is put into auxiliary details.

If you've found all of this, less then delightful, then the next chapter may be fitting!

CHAPTER 12

Prevention is better than cure

It feels a little counter-intuitive to have a Chapter about not wanting to breed, in a breeding book. If you had a false scare, the litter was unintentional or even intentional but enough to put you off for life. So I thought it should acknowledge how to prevent it from happening in future.

You need to take proactive steps to avoid such scenarios.

Female Cycle

A female is typically on heat for 3 weeks, reoccurring between every 6 to 12 months. Ideally, the male is kept away from the female during this time, particularly in the 2nd and 3rd week of her season.

The use of baby gates and dog cages will help but ultimately is not foolproof. Many persistent males will climb gates, even scaling fences and matings can still occur through cages. I've known dogs to mate while on their usual trip to the park, at a dog daycare and while in boarding kennels.

If you have a highly aroused male, it can be stressful for them. The constant pining can cause loss of condition and weight. In these instances, maybe the male living temporarily with friends or family would be easier.

Use can use anti-mate sprays and supplements to 'reduce' her attractiveness, along with dog knickers. These measures will not deter a determined mating pair. She should be kept housebound, and if exercised only on a leash, preferably with no other animals present.

'Morning after' medication

Well, it's not a pill as such. If you have knowingly seen a mating then a 'mismate' injection, called Alizin maybe required. A vet can administer the injection immediately, but no later than 45 days gestation. Alizin ensures the uterus cannot maintain pregnancy. Two doses must be given 24 hours apart.

Chemical Castration

This is a short term, temporary solution which can last between 6 to 12 month. The implant called Suprelorin induces temporary infertility in a male dog by reducing testosterone circulating in the blood.

The male will become infertile after about 6 weeks. You'll see a reduction in the size of his testicles, decreased libido and decrease sperm production, reducing the chances of pregnancy.

This is an ideal treatment for any show dogs which must be kept entire or dogs which may be considered for a future breeding programme. The majority of dogs regain normal semen characteristics approximately one year after the last treatment, but it's not guaranteed.

It's still advisable not to allow him to mate.

Permanent Choices

Both male and females can be neutered.

It's generally deemed easier to castrate a male, then a female due to the testicles being held outside the body. Either castrating a male or spaying a female will involve a general anaesthetic and is deemed a routine procedure, but any surgery will have an element of risk.

For this reason, I have known owners to spay their females when having a c-section. Opting for the traditional 'open spay' at the same time, so no additional surgeries are required. The uterus and ovaries are removed through the same c-section incision.

I have known breeders agree to this procedure with great success. Others have reservations on removing such hormonally charged reproductive tissues, so quickly after pregnancy and birth, with worries of the possible impacts on milk production. However, milk production is driven by the Pituitary Gland in the brain, not the ovaries. As a side note, umbilical hernias can also be repaired during c-section surgery.

'Lap spays' which are laparoscopic spay, mean they are conducted by keyhole surgery. You wouldn't do this at the same time as c-section, as there would be no benefits.

Should you decide to spay at any other time, typically 3 months after their last season, this method is far less invasive. The incisions to remove just the ovaries are much smaller than the alternative 'open spay' option. I have heard of vets spaying as young as 8 weeks old. Personally, my preference would be after the female has had her second season or last litter.

There is far less post-operative pain with a lapspay which leads to faster recovery time, then with open spays. Some bitches being exercised the next day and less pain medication required. Lap spays aren't typically offered by all veterinary practices because they may not have the appropriate equipment. This generally means Lapspays are more expensive to cover this additional cost.

I'll leave you do the research on the pros and cons and who is best to neuter, if not both, should you own both sexes.

There are charities such as Dog's Trust, offering to neuter at a hugely discounted price. The owner must be receiving benefits and the dog of a particular breed, or at least one of its parents. You'll find full details of participating vet practices through their website.

CHAPTER 13

So that's it

First congratulations with sticking with the book and making it to the end. This action itself has already set you apart from the majority of breeders.

This book has been crammed with all the tips and tools of the trade, which I've learnt since rearing my first litter in 1999, aged 17 years old. They have served me, and the people I have mentored well over the years.

You have certainly progressed. If you don't believe me name three things you know now, which didn't know before picking up and reading this book. If you can't think of any, then it says more about you then me. I strongly suggest you start back at the beginning, but this time make some notes or stick a star in the margins. This will remind you of some of the learning more relevant to you.

I'm twenty years in with breeding and my learning has never stopped, even attempting to keep pace with changes in the development of equipment, techniques and practises is enough to keep any experienced breeder on their toes.

If you are a new or novice breeder, then you no longer an 'Ostrich' with your head in the sand, concerning breeding. Reading this book has taken you on your first step of many in becoming a purposeful Home Breeder. You've now got the correct attitude and passion for implementing what you've learnt, ensuring you are successful in your breeding plans.

J.F.D.I

The hard work starts now, you know what you 'should' be doing. It's just you need to 'do it' Or JFDI, just focus and do it. I can't give you an exact, clear-cut plan or schedule of what you individually should do, because, for every breed, breeder and litter, the plan will be different.

The outline of your plan, however, is undoubtedly within the contents of this book, and just needs you to reflect and consider what they are and take action, now.

Want more help?

I have some special gifts for you as a committed reader of *'Not Born Yesterday'*. I'm hoping you've already managed to download your gifts that I've previously mentioned throughout the book. If you haven't, then the gifts are:

BONUS GIFT ONE: Whelping Wish List & Video - This breeder checklist is a full breakdown of the essential and 'nice to have' items needed to safely deliver puppies. Items are categorised by Maternity Unit/Whelping Area, Daily Consumables, Emergency Items, Dam & Puppy Care.

BONUS GIFT TWO: Dam's Diet Sheet & Video - Use this breeder help sheet to correctly increase the mother's food demands preventing over or underfeeding. The correct feeding will ensure suitably nourished puppies and reduce the chances of a difficult birth from oversized puppies.

BONUS GIFT THREE: Puppy Report Card & Video - Identify and track each puppy's individual progress, helping you to quickly acknowledge any failing or poorly puppies. Enabling you to make any relevant provisions to improve the survival rate.

These help sheets and supporting videos can be accessed through the **Home Breeder Hub.** The Hub is a haven where dog owners, united by the love for their four-legged folk who are dedicated to breeding. It's a mobile-friendly website where you can access vital information anywhere and anytime in addition to the bonus gifts.

I've arranged for you to have free access by registering at **www.caninefamilyplanner.com/NBY**

Home Breeder Puppy Playbook - The Sister Book

If you are seeking a more structured and supported approach to puppy rearing, then the **Home Breeders Puppy Playbook** may be for you.

It's a sister book helping you apply the knowledge you've gained from *Not Born Yesterday* by supporting you to make practical and beneficial decisions during your breeding journey.

The Playbook is supported by a **Puppy Pathway** within the Hub. The Puppy Pathway will take you from pre-mating until puppies are homed. The playbook includes the bonus gifts, plus additional advice and videos covering:

- Pre-mating preparations
- Stud Options
- Whelping Chart
- Birthing Planner
- Puppy Feeding Guide
- Puppy Meal Planner
- Puppy Socialisation checklist
- Vetting Questions & New owner log
- Template Receipt and Sales Contract
- Puppy Pack Checklist

The Playbook will also grant access to all the explanatory videos in the **Home Breeder Hub - Puppy Pathway**, where you can uncover a deeper level of detail into many of the breeding concepts and principles.

I've organised for you to have discounted upgrade by registering at **www.caninefamilyplanner.com/PLAYBOOK**

Home Breeder Hub - Very Important Breeder (ViB) Access

Regardless if you are new to breeding, an occasional breeder or feeling pretty competent, everyone likes to know there's someone that's got their back. In the Hub, I'm available to support and advise you, co-cry with you and share your successes. We all need reassurance as breeding can sometimes feel isolating and like being on an emotional rollercoaster.

The Home Breeder Hub's paid membership is the for contentious dog owners, who I like to call ViB's, Very Important Breeders. Breeder's who are looking for reliable support and advice, who yearn for a low stress whelping and rearing experience, producing healthy pups who are placed in good homes. If you are dedicated to investing in this pastime,then the Hub is the correct place for you.

What do you get as a ViB?

- Unlimited access to all resources in the Hub plus regularly newly added material
- Monthly printed and posted publication straight to your letterbox
- Private advice and support channel direct with me to discuss your dog's personal needs in detail
- Unrestricted Community forum access for more in-depth doggy discussions

You can register or upgrade your existing account for a readers discount offer, enabling superior access in just a few clicks of a button by visiting **www.caninefamilyplanner.com/VIB**

So what's stopping you? There's tons for you to be getting on with!

ABOUT THE AUTHOR

Moi?

So they say everyone has a book in them, I must admit I never thought my first would be advising owners on the byproduct of dog sex. When I look back, I'm not sure who's to blame for me achieving such titles as the 'scanning lady', 'dog w@nker' or 'canine family planner'.

At 6 years old, I remember the family trip to acquire our first family dog, a much-wanted Bulldog called Tina at the request of my keenest brother Clay. 30 years later and I've not spent more than 10 consecutive days away from the breed, so I guess they got me hooked?

I fell into the trap of 'Junior Handling' at a local dog training club, and I guess they say the rest is history.

After ditching University, I worked for 10 years in numerous corporate companies as a Learning & Development Consultant. When in 'the office' I'd have colleagues wanting updates on my weekend show wins and on 'training days' I'd have delegates wanting general 'doggy updates' and puppy pics. Not to mention local people who were used to seeing me making numerous dog walking trips, asking if I was a dog walker. I would confess "no, they are all my own" and I wasn't getting paid.

If I wasn't working or sleeping, I was doing something with a Bulldog, walking it, feeding it, training it, showing it or breeding it. That's were my passion evolved to a new level. When you show good dogs, people start approaching asking for advice and sometimes stud services, and that's where the first iteration of this book began.

Aged 13 and dying to get the full benefit of my Christmas present, my own 'personal computer'. This was when floppy discs were a thing, and access to the internet was dial-up.

I set to creating a 'Bulldog Breeding Bible' it was a simple weekly calendar with a notes section for any new and novice people to breeding. I had shown it to a few much more experienced breeders then my young self and they offered insightful, positive and encouraging feedback. I issued it to all bitch owners, who had used my stud dog, and that's how it stayed for many years.

It's said if you can breed Bulldogs, you can breed anything, they are so complicated and by chance that's exactly where I started. I decided after a redundancy to use some of the funds to buy a portable ultrasound machine. A service I had valued myself as a breeder, fast forward six years and I now offer a similar but more comprehensive Breeder service, from planning to pregnancy and newborn to new homes for my own like-minded community.

Nowadays I offer this information to a much wider variety of breed and breeders, pedigree, crossbred to designer dogs, pet and hobby breeders to licenced breeding kennels.

You'll notice this book doesn't cover the "birds and the bees" of dog breeding, or like most 'breeding books' whether you should actually mate or not. For the majority of people I come into contact with, the decision was made at least four weeks previous, or they might be dealing with an unintentional or unknown pregnancy.

This book is a deep dive into the reality of dealing with a pregnant dog. Advising how best you, as the owner and breeder of any puppies, should rear this new life — not shirking any breeder responsibilities and in fact, facing them head-on, by digesting the content of this book and taking appropriate action. Dog's Trust alone in 2018 cared for over 15,000 dogs, don't let yours be one of them, that's your *(and my)* ultimate duty.

Acknowledgements

These are the people I wish to give a metaphorical 'thank you' box of chocolates too.

Mummy Lamont, who has raised me to believe anything is possible if you're willing to give 100%. No matter how risky it looks or feels, she never fails to maintain her confidence in my abilities and never bats an eyelid at my sometimes crazy ideas.

My brothers who always ask about the dogs and know not to mention the 'C' word, Children to me.

Dominic Hodgson the UK's Leading Pet Business Coach and my mentor. He's everywhere, in my car, on my bookshelf, in my phone and PC, almost 'god-like' to me. He continually practises what he preaches, kicked my butt a few times to get this darn book finished and thus demands my respect and thanks.

To all the small business Pet Professionals, I collaborate with up and down the country. The struggle is real, but there isn't much better in life than being self-employed and working with dogs. FACT. We've got it good!

To all the LaRoyals who breezed breeding, Lexi and her famous litter of eleven. Not forgetting Roxi & Martin the proud parents of the most famous 'LaRoyal' aka Superstar, Lacey. My homebred Crufts Best of Breed Champion. Box ticked ;).

Alan Stewart, the only truly 'trusted' dog sitter when I was chasing and achieving the dog show dream; 'Top Bulldog 2013'. He also cooks a mean roast dinner, which was always appreciated after a long day dog showing.

My clients, for always having your bitches concerns at the forefront of your decisions. For sharing your experiences and knowledge with me, enabling me to develop a well-rounded and realistic perspective of breeding, helping me collate this book.

To you, the reader, for picking this book as one that's worth reading. Hopefully, you still agree now you've got to the end. It would be great if you can leave me a review, from wherever you purchased the book confirming as such. It might just convince me to write another.

I'm just an ordinary gal trying to make the world of dog breeding a slightly better place. If you think I've managed this, please share with like-minded people.

8·20·20

19·02	Black-white stripe on chest	9.75 onces.
20·15	Ginger-paler strip on head	9·2
22·01	Black-white on paws - white nose + tummy	9.8 Breach
	Ginger-paler than other one.	9·2
	Black	